Cambridge Elements

Elements in the Problems of God
edited by
Michael L. Peterson
Asbury Theological Seminary

GOD AND TECHNOLOGY

Heidi A. Campbell
Texas A&M University

CAMBRIDGE
UNIVERSITY PRESS

CAMBRIDGE
UNIVERSITY PRESS

Shaftesbury Road, Cambridge CB2 8EA, United Kingdom

One Liberty Plaza, 20th Floor, New York, NY 10006, USA

477 Williamstown Road, Port Melbourne, VIC 3207, Australia

314–321, 3rd Floor, Plot 3, Splendor Forum, Jasola District Centre,
New Delhi – 110025, India

103 Penang Road, #05–06/07, Visioncrest Commercial, Singapore 238467

Cambridge University Press is part of Cambridge University Press & Assessment,
a department of the University of Cambridge.

We share the University's mission to contribute to society through the pursuit of
education, learning and research at the highest international levels of excellence.

www.cambridge.org
Information on this title: www.cambridge.org/9781009507677

DOI: 10.1017/9781009287104

© Heidi A. Campbell 2025

This publication is in copyright. Subject to statutory exception and to the provisions
of relevant collective licensing agreements, no reproduction of any part may take
place without the written permission of Cambridge University Press & Assessment.

When citing this work, please include a reference to the DOI 10.1017/9781009287104

First published 2025

A catalogue record for this publication is available from the British Library

ISBN 978-1-009-50767-7 Hardback
ISBN 978-1-009-28709-8 Paperback
ISSN 2754-8724 (online)
ISSN 2754-8716 (print)

Cambridge University Press & Assessment has no responsibility for the persistence
or accuracy of URLs for external or third-party internet websites referred to in this
publication and does not guarantee that any content on such websites is, or will remain,
accurate or appropriate.

For EU product safety concerns, contact us at Calle de José Abascal, 56, 1°, 28003
Madrid, Spain, or email eugpsr@cambridge.org

God and Technology

Elements in the Problems of God

DOI: 10.1017/9781009287104
First published online: August 2025

Heidi A. Campbell
Texas A&M University

Author for correspondence: Heidi A. Campbell, heidic@tamu.edu

Abstract: This Element brings work from the philosophy of technology into conversation with media, religion, culture studies, and work in digital religion studies to explore examples of how popular media and emerging technologies are increasingly framed and understood through a distinct range of spiritual myths, metaphors, images, and representations of God. Working with case studies on how popular films and media coverage about AI connect to spiritual ideas, this Element draws attention to common conceptions that describe a perceived relationship between religion and technology today. It synthesizes these discussions and categories and presents them in four distinct models, showing a range of ways in which the relationship between God and technology is commonly depicted. The Element seeks to create a platform for scholarly study and critical discourse on technology's religious and spiritual representation in digital and emerging media cultures and contexts through this work.

This Element also has a video abstract:
www.cambridge.org/EPOG_Hcampbell_abstract

Keywords: technology, religion, AI, spirituality, God

ISBNs: 9781009507677 (HB), 9781009287098 (PB), 9781009287104 (OC)
ISSNs: 2754-8724 (online), 2754-8716 (print)

Contents

1 The Presence and Perception of God in a Technological World

Throughout history, religious impulses have often driven technological inventions' imagination and creative advances by inspiring inventors to dream and create new machines and innovations. In the 1840s, Samuel Morse evoked the divine when he typed out his first message on his ground-breaking invention, the telegraph; "What hath God wrought." Scholars have speculated that this response was inspired by Morse's contemplation of the superhuman potential that he created, allowing humans to transgress time and space communication in ways never before possible (Standage, 2014). Thirty years later, Alexander Graham Bell, an admitted agnostic, was said to have become speculative at the launch of his telephone and how its ability to capture the human voice and transmit it across time and space through physical wires in a way that he thought mimicked magic (Bruce, 1973). Later, Thomas Edison mixed his spiritual beliefs and inventive drive to bring forth the idea of the "spirit phone," an electric medium that would enable communication between the living and the dead (Martin, 2017). Whether attributed to God, pushing the boundaries of human ability, or even the realm of the spirit world, technologies have often readily evoked religious language and imagery.

A similar conceptual linking of the power and capabilities of technology to religion or religious-like manifestations by inventors also helped fuel the computer revolution. Computer architects imagined a powerful connection between the spiritual and material worlds they watched manifest through their work. Charles Babbage, a mathematician and father of the first mechanical computer, is argued to have seen religious beliefs and scientific pursuits as things that should be complementary and mutually supportive (Noble, 1999). Fast-forward a century, and in the 1990s, Steve Jobs, who was heavily influenced by his Zen Master, spoke openly about seeking to develop a spiritual rhythm between his computer design work and his Buddhist outlook to envision an "imaginative marriage of spiritual science and modern technology" (Robinson, 2013). This mindset helped him cultivate links between his work with the company Apple and his ideas of Buddhist enlightenment. This connection is seen in several Apple marketing promotions, such as its 1997 "Think Different" campaign and the 2007 "Touching is Believing" iPhone campaign. Such visible intersections of technology and religious imagery challenge arguments that science and religion are contradictory or competitive forces in direct opposition.

Thus, it can be argued that inventors, designers, and technology users across time have often employed narratives linking recent technologies to ideas of spirituality and religion and describe innovations as opening new doors to mystical experiences. This is especially true regarding current media discourses about artificial intelligence and how some see this emerging technology as a new form of religion. As this Element argues, The use of religious language and imagery to describe the perceived power and potential of modern technologies is in no way a new trend. Numerous examples can be found in literature and philosophical writings over the last two centuries, which consciously connect technology to ideas about religion and spirituality.

This Element, *God and Technology*, explores diverse ways ideas about religion, spirituality, and technology have intersected or been connected within scholarly literature, popular media, and public discourse about recent technologies. It specifically looks at the historical roots of common metaphors and conceptual connections used to describe and equate aspects of contemporary technologies to ideas of God. A central argument of this brief Element is that the God-like imagery and qualities often attributed to the internet, digital cultures, mobile technologies, and artificial intelligence emerge from a deeply rooted discourse rooted in distinctive Western views about science, technology, and the human condition. This Element seeks to draw attention to the origins of these connections and broaden this perspective by showing that while contemporary discourse about technology heavily relies on Western religious beliefs about God, twenty-first-century framings of technology are increasingly drawing on multi-religious metaphors and beliefs to describe the god-like or spiritual nature of technology.

This Element highlights the common symbols and metaphors used by both scholarly and popular writers to express connections between God and technology, as well as show how and where these ideas are manifest in contemporary media depictions of technology and what influence different representations have on public beliefs and discussions about technology. Overall, *God and Technology* provides a brief investigation and overview of the primary images and ideas about God and religion associated with and applied to technology and how this informs how we see both the potential and problems technology poses to humanity and our future. The main aim of this work is to spotlight core discourses and conceptual ideas used to talk about technology in religious terms. *God and Technology* introduces these common categories to scholars to create a platform for more rigorous discussion and fruitful study about how widespread religious and spiritual representation of technology shapes our understanding, interactions, and expectations of emerging technologies.

Contextualizing My Approach to God and Technology

By exploring the ideas and images about God, religion, and spirituality used to epitomize technology, this work brings the Philosophy of Technology into conversation with Digital Religion Studies. Digital Religion studies is an emerging area of scholarship that I have helped pioneer and develop. It seeks to show how religious beliefs and practices from established offline institutions and communities intersect with different expressions of spirituality and religiosity found in technologically mediated contexts.

It is important to note that while this Element is situated in a philosophy-focused series, it is not written by a philosopher. As an interdisciplinary scholar who has researched and written for over three decades on topics at the intersection of media, religion, and culture, I draw on work from multiple disciplines, including the study of Communication, Philosophy, Religion, Sociology, and Theology. In Philosophy, my expertise is limited to the Philosophy of Technology and Science and Ethics of Communication and Media Technologies. I acknowledge that this may be seen as a significant limitation of the Element to some readers. There are some sections of this Element where a deeper dive into Philosophical concerns could be taken. However, that is beyond the overall focus of this text and my expertise. I believe my work in the Philosophy of Technology, along with the breadth of my interdisciplinary background, proves to be an asset for exploring the specific topic of *God and Technology*.

Also, while the focus of the Elements series is on "The Problem of God," *God and Technology* does not take a traditional approach to this question, instead focusing on some of the common Philosophically oriented concerns evoked by this question – such as debates about the existence of God, how God is framed as a theoretical entity, or exploring different cultural conceptions of God – this Element focuses on identifying and defining how God is depicted and framed as theoretical entity when discussed or described about ideas of technology.

Further, *God and Technology* argues that historically, when discussions of conceptions of God have been evoked about technology, these ideas about God are typically rooted in Western Judeo-Christian discourses and understandings of God. Much of the previous work looking at the relationship between God and technology in the Philosophy of Technology and Media Studies or Religious Communication is often based on an underlying assumption of a monotheistic God, a perspective often unrecognized or uninterrogated. However, in the past two decades, a rise in scholarship has begun to recognize the limits of this perspective, especially in a global, multicultural society (Bunt, 2009; Grieve & Veidlinger, 2014; Zeiler, 2019).

God and Technology recognizes the prevalence of this default understanding of God when technology is described as having god-like qualities or tendencies and seeks to provide a more robust discussion about the vision of god truly being presented by carefully examining the metaphors and comparisons made in contemporary media depictions of God. This is done by distinguishing different understandings of God in the text by using the terms God (Western Monotheistic understanding), god/s or deities (polytheistic understanding), and transcendent spirit (nontheistic understanding). These differentiations are discussed more below in the section called "God in Context." It is recognized that there are still limitations to using these distinctions. Arguably, more reflection needs to be given to issues of how embedded Western assumptions about religion have limited discussions of God and technology. However, this interrogation is beyond the limits of this Element. However, I hope that by raising this issue in the text and attempting to offer a slightly more nuanced approach to discussions of "God," this Element will open space for future work in this area.

While many means could be used to tackle and unpack the relationship between God and technology, this text focuses on specific approaches around the historical and contemporary use of religious imagery and language used to represent aspects of the supernatural and divine about technology. However, some background and contextual work is needed before discussing how religion is used to discuss and describe technology.

Studying Religious Intersections with Technology

One strand of my research over the past three decades has focused on identifying the prominent ways that religion and technology interact, especially through the social-technical infrastructure of our Western culture that has become heavily reliant on computer technology and networking. Using a variety of case studies and forms of media analysis, I have shown that each new generation of technology draws on religious images, ideas, and impulses to help market, advocate for, and explain the functions of new forms of both digital and mobile media. It has not been difficult to gather various examples of how digital devices are often framed using religious ideals or equated with theological conceptions like salvation or divinity. In this Element, I will discuss some examples I have studied. In the past two decades, I have undertaken a dozen different studies exploring the variety of ways technology has been connected to spiritual beliefs and how these instances can be understood or interpreted. My research has studied how religious imagery and texts attribute spiritual qualities to various communication technologies. This includes how technology creators and companies use religious symbols to market and communicate the potential of smartphones (Campbell & LaPastina, 2010), the ways popular media – such as films – attribute certain religious-like beliefs to emerging technologies (Campbell, 2016), and how human interactions with digital media make visible certain spiritual assumptions about the relationship between humans and technology (Campbell, 2021).

From this work, I argue that using religious symbols creates a unique language pointing to several common underlying spiritual myths about technology within our contemporary media culture. These discussions regarding the conceptual relationship between religion and technology can and should take place both in popular media culture and within various academic disciplines. I argue that it is crucial to truly consider these discourses in both spaces to understand the spiritual and religious impulses of our current technological culture. In this Element, I discuss the religious ideas regarding how God is defined and understood, which have been attributed and communicated within digital media culture.

Through research, I have observed that using religious language and images in public discourse about technology is common. Religious metaphors have been used to communicate positive and negative views about technology. Ideas about God and divinity are often evident in these discussions. I have argued that popular discussions about technology rely on certain stories and myths that reveal how God is conceived of in contemporary culture and how engagement with digital media culture can be seen as a spiritual pursuit. Because much of the Western world is immersed and wrapped in technology, it can be hard to see the specific ways that narratives about technology shape our view of reality, shape our view of the natural world, and suggest certain spiritual beliefs. In the following pages, I explore ways God is represented and defined within our digitally driven spaces and contexts, revealing the dominant narratives that inform the spiritual outlook of our technological world.

In the rest of Section 1, I discuss the role of ideas about God in previous studies in the philosophy of technology and current popular media conversations. This foundational understanding allows us to consider the influence that religious discourse has in shaping the current understanding of digital media and AI developments. Also, as a heavily conceptual and nuanced topic, it is important to define key terms and their interrelationships regarding how technology, religion, and God are understood in this work.

Defining Technology

It is important to begin with a brief discussion of how the concept of technology is approached in the Element. Defining technology can be complex due to its roots and how its meaning has evolved.

The modern word *technology* originates from the Greek *technology* (τεχνολογία), composed of *techne* (τέχνη) and *logica* (λογία). In ancient Greek thought, *technologia* broadly referred to the systematic study (*logica*) of practical arts and skills (*techne*), unlike its modern association with machinery and innovation. Instead, it pertained to discussions on craftsmanship, artistry, and techniques used in skilled trades (Salomon, 1984). Unpacking the terms *techne* and *logica* is important for understanding the historical evolution of ideas around technology.

Techne (τέχνη) – which is often translated as "art," "craft," or "skill" – was a key concept in Greek philosophy. Aristotle distinguished *techne* from *episteme* (scientific knowledge), emphasizing its practical nature (Aristotle 1094a–1095a). The term was applied to fields like sculpture, medicine, and shipbuilding, reflecting its role in producing artifacts through learned skills. Plato treated *techne* as structured knowledge that distinguished skilled labor from mere manual activity (Plato 601d). This understanding shaped early Western technology ideas by highlighting craftsmanship and the intentional application of knowledge to its meaning. *Logica* (λογία), derived from *logos* (λόγος), signifies "word," "reason," or "discourse." A foundational Greek concept, *logos* represented rationality and structured argumentation. Heraclitus and Aristotle used *logos* to describe the rational order of the universe and human reasoning (Jaeger, 1944). When combined with *techne*, *technologia* initially referred to the systematic study of practical skills (Robinson, 1969).

During the medieval period, *technologia* was rarely used, as knowledge was classified under philosophy, theology, and mechanical arts. During the Renaissance period, scholars revived Greek ideas, and by the seventeenth century, scholars such as Francis Bacon and René Descartes redefined knowledge, emphasizing empirical science (Bacon, 1620). *Technologia* began appearing in Latin texts, influencing the modern understanding of technology. *Technology* was introduced into the English language in the seventeenth century, originally denoting the systematic study of the mechanical arts (Kline, 2003; Schatzberg, 2006). During the nineteenth century, the Industrial Revolution significantly broadened its meaning, shifting from focusing on theoretical study to encompassing the practical application of scientific knowledge in industrial processes and technological innovations (Schatzberg, 2006). This transformation reflected the growing intersection between science, engineering, and economic production, which became central to modern technological development (Kline, 2003).

By the early twentieth century, technology became associated with machines, industrial processes, and engineering. Philosophers such as Thorstein Veblen examined technology as a driving force in economic and social change (Veblen, 1921). Later philosophers such as Martin Heidegger explored the deeper existential and societal implications of technology, arguing modern technological development transforms not only the material world but also human ways of being (Heidegger, 1958). Today, *technology* is often used for new scientific innovations or technological devices, such as digital computing, artificial intelligence, and biotechnologies.

While the word technology still retains its connection to *techne* (practical skill) and *logica* (systematic knowledge), the modern understanding of technology often centers around the idea of physical tools (Salomon, 1984). Yet the growing complexity of living in a digital culture wrapped in media means these tools include computer systems, network infrastructures, and a growing number of augmented and virtual realities. This brief exploration of the word technology reflects humanity's changing understanding of knowledge and tools and how humans have had to progressively adapt to new intellectual and material contexts in society. Understanding this history helps us see that technology is a term that includes the idea of tools, techniques, and the application of certain kinds of knowledge within it. In this Element, the term "technology" refers to current and emerging digital devices and computer-driven innovation, which carry a distinct logic that predisposes them to certain framings and associations with religion and spirituality.

Within the Philosophy of Technology study, there is an acknowledgment that humans have often equated or at least associated technological artifacts with religious-like language, qualities, and experience. Technology is often framed not as a neutral tool but as part of a value-laden enterprise with social and moral implications (Campbell, 2010). Because of this, many philosophers and theorists, when exploring technology, have employed spiritual language and concepts to describe and debate the values of power, control, and efficiency, all promoted by technology. For example, Martin Heidegger argued in his book *The Question Concerning Technology* that any human attempt to control technology can be a spiritual act. This, he suggested, is because technology offers humans a form of salvation, rescuing us from the weaknesses and pitfalls of the human condition. Scholars such as Karl Marx and Walter Benjamin, who are discussed more in the next section, have also written about the promises and perils of technology using religious-like undertones and language to support their arguments. Also, it is important that science fiction literature and film – as discussed in Section 2 of the Element – have played an important role in shaping contemporary understanding of technology and coupled it with spiritual ideals. William Gibson's sci-fi novel *Neuromancer* (1984) was foundational in defining the popular idea of cyberspace in the 1990s as a Cartesian dualistic escape from the human body and the "real world" to an enhanced life beyond the screen. His work presented the future digital world as a place of transcendent hope for humanity, using gnostic spiritual images and beliefs to support this myth. (DiTommaso, 2011). Becoming aware of how religion has been and is used to describe praise and even critique technology helps to discern the common conceptual relationships presented about God and technology.

The Values of Technology

It is important to understand not only how the concept of technology is defined and the different ways it is conceived in contemporary culture. Technologies are not just tools or techniques that help humans perform specific tasks; as expressed earlier, they are knowledge embedded with distinct values and affordances. Ivan Illich, in his book *Tools of Conviviality* (1973), offers a distinctive argument about the values that should motivate and drive technological development, which has informed my thinking about the character of technology. In his book, Illich writes about creating a bicycle-based transportation system for the developing world, composed of a series of human-powered vehicles, which benefit both the health of its users and the transport needs of the culture. For him, a bicycle-based transport system represents technology that is not simply a tool that performs a task but a device that creates a culture around it. He argues that technologies are best when a device's design and default use create a supportive relationship between a human user and the artifact. According to Illich, convivial technology represents:

> ... tools, technologies & infrastructures for enacting the public commons in open, enlivening ways. They foster relations within and beyond the human world and bring about small, slow, and simple energy-efficient solutions. (Genovese & Pansera, 2019, p. 12)

In other words, a convivial tool is mutually beneficial; it should be adapted to serve human needs and used in ways that do not degrade the environment or society. Illich believed a bicycle is convivial because it supports human needs for movement and transportation but does not inherently introduce by-products or encourage patterns of use that would adversely affect the earth.

He also stated that computers or software programs are not convivial technologies because they promote problematic human patterns and values. Like Jacques Ellul, Illich argued that the modern technological enterprise is based on several core problematic values, which I believe have driven much of the advancement of digital, mobile, and robotic technologies. At the root of this is the idea that humanity is flawed and needs to be fixed or improved upon. This has promoted a technological industry fueled by efficiency, progress, and mastery. It is one based on individualism rather than a communal mindset.

Where do these values originate from? Scholars have argued that many core values of our information society are by-products of the cultural and technological developments of the Industrial Revolution of the 1800s (Castells, 1997;

Ong, 2012). The creation of factories in urban centers proved profitable as owners emphasized increased productivity and capital accumulation fueled by technological improvements and the rise of standardized production processes within these factories (Beniger, 2009). The technological enterprise today, in large part, is based on three core values promoted and then refined by the work of American inventor Henry Ford in his model for the assembly line plan. Ford's early twentieth-century manufacturing model drove much of American technological expansion and production throughout World Wars I and II (Boynton & Milazzo, 1996). The Fordist model of production was based on three key traits:

> the standardization of products,
> the intensification of the labor process, and
> the specialized equipment and assembly lines increases productivity
>
> (Wanjiru, 2015).

First, the standardization of factories and their products leads to streamlining resources and cost-effective production. This standardization promoted efficiency as a key value. Next, the intensification of labor refers to the breaking down the production process. Instead of each worker building a complete product, labor processes were broken down into focused tasks, with each factory worker performing a single task related to the overall production of the product. This created a production process emphasizing the value of individualism, where an individual's actions are emphasized as the focal point of work rather than creating a unified project. Individual workers became specialized and absorbed into performing highly focused assigned tasks. Finally, specialized equipment and technologies were created and integrated into the factories to help support this task-focused form of production. This further detached the workers from the overall product being created so that they focused only on their specific assignment. This specialization of tasks encouraged an environment of constant refinement and worker mastery over individualized tasks. This refinement or progress became an ideal good and goal for factories (Boynton & Milazzo, 1996). Ford's assembly line production – and its accompanying core values of efficiency, individualism, and progress – were so successful that this production model evolved into a recognized economic-labor system known as Fordism (Roobeek, 1987). Fordism and its ingrained values of efficiency, individualism, and progress became a central ideological model that has continued to drive technological innovation and advancement into the current era.

While much more could be said about Fordism's historical roots and implications, what is most important for our purpose here is to emphasize that these values of efficiency, progress, and individualism are still central and highly visible in twenty-first-century technological culture. In many respects, they have often gone unquestioned as the driving ideals motivating and shaping the computer, internet, smart technology, and revolutions. They have and continue to serve as an often invisible and ingrained trajectory pushing, especially Western capitalist production processes, and create a platform for the global information society that has embraced digitization and a technologically embedded culture (Whitman, 2004). While a full mapping and unpacking of how these three values inform twenty-first-century society is not possible in this Element. it is important to name and acknowledge the influence of these values of technology. This discussion helps us to discuss some of the foundational and innate conflicts that arise when religious beliefs and traditions intersect with technology.

So, how do we approach technology as a value-laden artifact? It begins by realizing there is more than one way that technology can be perceived as having value, and that value informs its use. Along these lines, McOmber (1999) said technologies are defined by one of three common discourses. Each offers a different narrative about how technology develops and its societal role. The first story presents technology as a form of "instrumentality" and focuses on the fact that technology exists to perform a certain task in the service of a specific culture (pg. 141). This emphasizes that technology has a clear role and one it was designed for. Technologies are thus seen as being neither inherently good nor bad; they are neutral, and their value is designated by how they are used and the outcome of their use. Yet technology as instrumentality does recognize that technologies do not exist within a cultural vacuum; they emerge within a distinctive culture and time, so they can influence and inform that same culture in which they exist. For example, a hammer may be described as a simple tool created to help pound nails into wood, enabling humans to build structures or other objects. The existence of the hammer then enables humans to build new kinds of shelter that protect them from the natural elements. This instrumental nature of the hammer helps humans create new structures and a new culture of house-building. Still, the instrumental view of technology primarily emphasizes a neutral view of technology that accepts its ubiquity in culture and is ambivalent about its development.

Next, McOmber suggests that technology can be seen as a force behind industrialization. Here, technology is often associated with the Industrial Revolution of the eighteenth and nineteenth centuries in Western Europe and America and the rise of mass production. This definition emphasizes that technology "is the product of a specific historical time and place" so that "Technology is as much an event as a set of practices or objects" (pg. 143). This perspective connects to the Marxist view of history and the Political

Economy theory approach within Media Studies. Karl Marx argued that technology drives historical change by shaping the economic foundation of society (MacKenzie, 1984). He believed that modern technologies create new production processes, disrupt existing social structures, and create inequities in society. Marx's ideas influenced the rise of Political Economy theory in media studies, which examines and explores how economic and power structures shape media content and reinforce social inequalities. The owners and power brokers behind communication media use this technology to enact certain societal power dynamics (Pivetti, 2015). Technology as industrialization presents a very pessimistic view of technology (Mitcham & Mackey, 1971). This is exemplified by scholars like Jacques Ellul, who argued in *The Technological Society* (1964) that technology prioritizes efficiency over human values and ultimately controls society, leading to unintended and dehumanizing consequences. Thus, this definition of technology assumes that technology equals industrialization, and so should be viewed with suspicion and approached with criticism.

Finally, McOmber (1999) introduces us to the definition of technology as novelty, drawing heavily on the idea that technology is a by-product of human imagination and part of a continuously evolving process of creativity. This perspective focuses on technological innovation and "implies a narrative of development that is not wholly continuous or discontinuous" (McOmber 144). Technologies come and go; new inventions replace and displace older ones. This presents technologies as entities that are part of the broader life cycle. McOmber suggests this definition is often employed by technological optimists, who are attracted to the cult of the new, are driven toward change, and see constant development and refinement as a foregone conclusion. This, he argues, promotes a highly idealized view of "progress" and an "ahistorical" outlook, as "history begins with the latest technological breakthrough, and one need not extend the narrative of development backward to discover the cultural origins of the latest panacea" (pg. 145). This technology as novelty viewpoint, can come across as overly positive about the potential of technology.

In summary, technology as instrumentality views technology as a neutral tool designed to perform specific tasks within a cultural context, influencing but not inherently shaping society, with its value determined by its use and outcomes. Technology as industrialization frames technology as a historical force tied to industrialization, emphasizing its role in shaping economic structures, reinforcing power dynamics, and often leading to societal disruptions and inequalities. Finally, technology as novelty sees technology as an evolving product of human creativity, promoting an idealized, ahistorical belief in continuous progress and innovation, often disregarding historical context and cultural origins. McOmber's three narratives provide a helpful spectrum of views about technology that have embedded within it neutral, pessimistic, and optimistic views of the value and impact of technology on society. This range of perspectives will be used as discussion tools in this Element to help highlight the general outlook and values assumptions of different religious metaphors and myths about technology highlighted in this text.

God in Context

Defining God is a complex endeavor, as conceptions of the divine vary widely across religious traditions. In general, the term "god" refers to a supernatural being or revered deity, but in many religious traditions, *God* – with a capital "G" – signifies an ultimate, transcendent entity central to faith and worship (Armstrong, 1993). Understanding how different religions conceptualize God requires examining the theological frameworks of the world's major traditions: Christianity, Islam, Judaism, Hinduism, and Buddhism.

Monotheistic religions – such as Judaism, Christianity, and Islam – affirm belief in one God who is supreme, eternal, and distinct from creation. Judaism, the oldest of the three Abrahamic traditions, views God (YHWH) as an indivisible, covenantal deity who revealed divine law to Moses (Levenson, 2006). While affirming monotheism, Christianity introduces the doctrine of the Trinity, wherein God exists as Father, Son, and Holy Spirit (McGrath, 2011). Islam similarly upholds strict monotheism (*tawhid*), emphasizing God's absolute oneness (*Allah*) and transcendence, as revealed in the Qur'an (Esposito, 2018).

Hinduism, however, offers a pluralistic understanding of the divine, encompassing polytheistic, henotheistic, and monotheistic elements. Many Hindus believe in a supreme, unchanging reality (*Brahman*) that manifests through multiple deities such as Vishnu, Shiva, and Devi (Flood, 1996). The *Bhagavad Gita* illustrates this complexity, describing Krishna as a personal deity and an expression of the ultimate divine (Flood, 1996). Unlike the Abrahamic and Hindu traditions, Buddhism does not center on a creator God. Instead, it focuses on the teachings of the Buddha, emphasizing enlightenment (*nirvana*) through ethical living and meditation. While some Buddhist traditions incorporate divine beings, ultimate reality is understood through the *Dharma* rather than a deity (Harvey, 2013). These diverse perspectives make discussions about God in contemporary culture and technology particularly complex, as the very definition of God varies widely across traditions.

Christian theological concepts often subtly shape conversations surrounding technology in the twenty-first century. This is no accident; being the dominant religious tradition in the West, Christianity has deeply influenced the cultural landscape from which our digital technologies and AI innovations emerge

(Borgman, 2003). Discussions about technology frequently, if implicitly, draw upon monotheistic understandings of God. For example, the idea of a single, all-powerful creator God resonates with the concept of a single, ultimate source code, central computer, or a powerful AI. Discourse in the scholarly study of religion and science has also contributed to making conceptual linkages between God and religion. For those in Christianity who understand God to be the ultimate "intelligent designer" of the universe, this suggests the idea that human technology developers should be seen as creators of these complex technological systems (Demski, 2002). Such representation also mirrors the Judeo-Christian concept of *imago Dei*, the idea that humans are made in God's image, thus possessing creative capacities (Jantzen, 1995).

Furthermore, the language of "miracles" is often applied to technological breakthroughs, evoking a sense of divine intervention and wonder. While these parallels are rarely explicitly theological, they demonstrate how deeply ingrained religious frameworks are in our understanding and articulation of technology. This underscores the importance of recognizing these implicit connections to foster more nuanced and critical discussions about the role of technology in our lives.

Yet, while Western discussions of technology often implicitly draw on Christian concepts of God, eastern religious traditions are increasingly influencing how technology is perceived and discussed in twenty-first-century media culture and at innovation hubs like Silicon Valley. This influence extends beyond mere philosophical interest; tech companies frequently invite gurus to speak on mindfulness and technology, and some even employ Buddhist monks as spiritual advisors (Bao, 2005). Hindu concepts like interconnectedness and the cyclical nature of time resonate with the networked structure of the internet and the rapid pace of technological change. The idea of *maya*, the illusory nature of reality, can be seen reflected in discussions of virtual reality and the blurring lines between the physical and digital worlds. Similarly, Buddhist principles of mindfulness and meditation are increasingly integrated into tech culture to manage stress and enhance productivity, even being incorporated into app designs (Samuel, 2023). The concept of emptiness (*sunyata*) in Mahayana Buddhism, which emphasizes the interconnectedness and impermanence of all things, can be seen as analogous to technology's fluid and ever-changing nature. These examples illustrate how Hindu and Buddhist philosophies influence individual practices within the tech industry and shape the language and metaphors used to understand and discuss technology's role in our lives. Some scholars even argue that these nontheistic understandings of religion are gaining prominence over traditional theistic conceptions of God in our increasingly technologized world (Chen, 2022). This integration of

Eastern thought highlights the diverse spiritual landscape shaping contemporary technological discourse.

This trend is noted in this Element, recognizing that monotheistic and nontheistic religious discourses are prevalent and evoked in different technology discussions. Therefore, when the term God with a capital G is used in the text, it references a monotheistic view of a singular deity. This specifically draws on Jewish and Christian or Judeo-Christian beliefs about the character and role of God from the Jewish Torah and/or the Christian Bible. When the term god with a "small g" is used, it is about polytheistic notions of the existence of multiple gods who may differ in their character and goals. Nontheistic religious views, especially ideas drawn from Buddhism about the afterlife and the ultimate reality of our world, are also found in discussions of religion and technology.

Contextualizing Religion and Spirituality about Technology

Until this point, the term "religion" has been used to describe recognized belief systems. It has also been connected to a specific religious tradition associated with a distinct conceptualization of God and other supernatural deities (i.e., Judaism, Islam, Christianity, Hinduism) or a pattern of life guided by certain religious teachings (i.e., Buddhism, Daoism). In this Element, attention is paid to how God/gods are represented in popular media by employing images of god from various religious traditions. However, understanding religion as an organized system of beliefs or oriented around a specific community of practice is not the only way to conceptualize religion. Indeed, scholars of religion have long debated what the term "religion" means and how expressions of "the religious" should be classified (McCutcheon, 2018).

Drawing on conversations in Religious Studies, religion can be conceptualized in broader and more dynamic ways than traditional definitions focused solely on belief in deities. Scholars like Robert Bellah (1970) suggest religion can be understood as patterns of devotion and meaning-making that shape how people understand and act. At its foundation, religion often involves a deep conviction about something that transcends ordinary reality – whether that's a divine being, an ultimate truth, or a transformative force. Thomas Luckmann (1967) describes this as an "invisible religion" when beliefs and convictions about the transcendent aspect of life don't have to be tied to the supernatural. Rather, religion offers organizing principles that help people find meaning and purpose. From these core convictions emerge what Catherine Albanese calls a "cultural system" – sets of beliefs, practices, and rituals that express and reinforce people's commitments. Religion scholars like Robert Bellah (1970) suggest we look at religion as patterns of devotion and meaning-making that shape how people understand and act. At its foundations, religion often involves a deep conviction about something that transcends ordinary reality – whether that's a divine being, an ultimate truth, or a transformative force. While traditional definitions of religion focus on formal institutions and supernatural beliefs, contemporary scholars help us see religion as a more fluid phenomenon that combines meaningful convictions about reality with corresponding ways of living and acting in the world.

Two contemporary understandings become central in looking at the relationship between religion and technology, as explored in this Element. These are "lived religion" and "implicit religion." Lived religion focuses on how individual practitioners interpret and live out their core religious beliefs and rituals. David Hall (1997) has argued that individuals in contemporary Western culture may affiliate with a specific religious tradition but often adapt traditional beliefs and behaviors to their life patterns. Therefore, lived religion may differ slightly or significantly from the official teachings of religious institutions or leaders. Nancy Ammerman's (2006) research on "everyday religion" also argues religious beliefs and practices become malleable as they are woven into daily life, creating new patterns of religious behavior that reflect people's deepest values and sense of ultimate meaning. Scholars studying digital religion have similarly argued that the individualized focus and empowerment of digital media platforms often encourage religious individuals to practice their religion in individualized and heterodoxical ways (Aguilar et al., 2017; Bellar et al., 2013). Awareness of this approach to religion is important for discussions in Section 2, where popular understandings of God are often filtered through the lens of lived religion. This creates new and novel re-presentations of the divine that may counter traditional presentations.

Another relevant approach to studying religious understandings of technology is "implicit religion." Implicit religion acknowledges that as contemporary society becomes more secular in its focus, individuals seek alternative arenas to derive purpose and a sense of belonging (Bailey, 1997). While people may look for alternatives to religious institutions in contemporary culture, they often still seek experiences that fulfill a desire for transcendence, belief, and rituals (Bellah, 1970). Implicit religion, also referred to as invisible religion (Luckman, 1967) and para- or quasi-religion (Griel, 1993), is an important concept because scholars have argued that many individuals in the twenty-first century have begun to see technology and treat its use as a form of religion. Scholars have written about how technology brands, like Apple, have achieved cult-like status among their fans due to ardent users' devotion to their devices (i.e., Campbell & LaPastina, 2010; Robinson, 2015). Others have argued that the way people devote time and energy to emerging technologies like the internet, social media, or artificial intelligence, technology has become a god-like entity (Campbell, 2016b; Singler, 2020). Understanding implicit religion is important in this Element because of the discussions in Sections 3 and 4, in which technology is often described and depicted using religious symbols and concepts to present technological engagement as a spiritual exercise. Also, when the term "religious-like" is used in this Element, I am referring to the understanding of technology practice or experience as a form of implicit religion.

Spirituality is a concept often associated with the discussion of religion, and like the term "religion," its core definition is often contested. Historically, the term was first used about belief in the existence of a divine "spirit" or the supernatural at work in the world. For example, in the Christian tradition, spirituality was linked to the notion of the "holy spirit," one manifestation of the triune understanding of God. The belief is that this spirit was in communion with humanity to draw them closer to God. Over time, spirituality began to be associated with the practical or applied side of religion and religious pursuits (Principe, 1983). Spirituality has become a broad term to describe the human pursuit of the transcendent or attempts to engage in existential levels of reality. It is often used as a catch-all concept to describe seeking to understand the spiritual side of life, whether it is one informed by a given religious tradition or a more general awareness of there being something beyond the world of the five senses. In this Element, spirituality describes the pursuit of a lived reality and/or transcendent experience, connected with the first of three categories discussed above that make up the core of religion. However, the connection of spirituality to the idea of religion is more strongly associated with the concept of "lived religion" than the concept of religion derived from a tradition. Like lived religion, spirituality focuses on living out one's belief with concrete and visible manifestations of practice drawn from specific beliefs. Spirituality is used in this Element about technology to focus on how individuals express their religious beliefs in their everyday lives, whether derived from a monotheistic or nontheistic understanding of god.

Relationship between God and Technology

In bringing these brief discussions about technology, religion, and God into conversation, it is important to note that the relationships between these concepts have an evolving history of connections and tensions. In the Epilogue to *Thinking through Technology* (1994), Carl Mitcham asserts that Western beliefs about technology can be seen as a continuum of responses marked by dominant philosophical outlooks used to frame the Sciences during distinct historical periods. He first introduces a period described as "Ancient Skepticism," beginning in the pre-modern world. He argues that this period held a general suspicion about technology and created artifacts that did not emerge from the natural world. This technological skepticism centers on the assumption that technology, because it is created and therefore outside the natural order of the world, inherently disrupts it. Thus, during this period, it was believed that technical proficiency tended to lead humanity away from the natural world and its reliance on God. Technology is thus seen as creating a trajectory that leads humanity away from ancient truths, faith in God, and connection to the natural world.

This move is credited with giving rise to the era of Enlightenment and "scientific optimism," which is said to promote an overly positive view of technology (Mitcham, 1994). Here, the focus is placed on the human relationship with technology, where technical skills offer unique potential for human advancement and socialization. Technology and the scientific enterprise helped build a new project or view of society. Scientific optimism frames technological innovation as the solution to most societal ills and shortcomings. Within this viewpoint, technology is framed as being ordained by God for the betterment of humanity. So, technology becomes privileged and empowered within this culture in a new way.

The polar extremes between technological suspicion and optimism gave way to what Mitcham (1994) describes as romantic uneasiness about technology. This highlighted a growing uncertainty about the implications of a world centered around the human-created process of technology and science and their tendency to supplant traditional relationships and boundaries between God, the natural world, and the scientific model of reality. Scholars have reflected on how this period led to both the rise of the Industrial Revolution's new era of mass production and growing fears about how these technologies give rise to monsters of our own making that may, in the end, destroy the humanity of the natural world (i.e., Ong, 2012). According to Coookolborgh (2017), this romantic uneasiness about technology created a dialectical tension about the power and path of emerging machines that still exist today. Consequently, Mitchum (1994) asserts a "middle-of-the-road" ambivalence toward technology emerged, focusing on the influence of the technical on human culture. Over time, this technological ambivalence has led to a more critical reflection on the social and cultural impact of the industrial revolution. Attention shifts to the benefits technology offers humanity, weighing against the real-life social consequences its embrace creates on the natural world. The result is that technology is seen as both a powerful symbol of human creativity and a tool of human destruction because technology is often developed at the expense of virtues that benefit all humanity.

This point is raised in the book *The Question Concerning Technology*, where Heidegger makes three primary claims about the nature of technology. First, he argues that technology is "not an instrument" but a way of understanding the world. Thus, technology can be seen as a value-laden enterprise that informs our view of the human world, much like religion offers specific perspectives and interpretive frames. Second, technology is "not a human activity" because it can develop beyond human control. This means that while humans may initially create a technology, the values and dispositions inserted into it may lead to unexpected developments or consequences. Third, Heidegger argues that technology is "the highest danger" because it directs the human gaze to only see the world through technological thinking. In this respect, he suggests technology can become like a religion by offering individuals a belief system, purpose, and framework for interpreting the world.

Many scientists and theologians agree that there is a close connection between and even a co-dependence of science/technology and religion (Padget, 2005). For example, Albert Einstein is quoted as having said, "Science without religion is lame. Religion without Science is blind." Thomas Merton, a Trappist monk and modern-day mystic, is attributed to the saying, "Technology in and of itself is not opposed to spirituality and religion. But it is a great temptation." Other scholars have alluded to the promise and perils of technology with religious-like undertones when presenting technology as a powerful force that controls and liberates people (Borgmann, 2003). This Element recognizes this and seeks to unpack the common ways technology has been linked with religious ideas, language, and images, consider how conceptions of God and gods are evoked in these discussions, and offer us both useful and problematic understandings of humanity's relationship to technology.

Mapping the Conversation in *God and Technology*

It can be challenging to talk about the existence and conceptions of God in contemporary culture. Similarly, inserting God into conversations about technology is no less difficult. To explore ways ideas about God emerge within current media discourses, this Element offers three brief case studies demonstrating how religious rhetoric has been used to evoke certain ideas about technology's divine and supposed spiritual nature. The Element also demonstrates that the deliberate use of distinct religious images and concepts shapes many current discussions about our communicative, informational, and biological technologies and the cultures they create around them.

This first section of the Element, "The Presence and Perception of God in a Technological World," has sought to introduce the foundational concepts – God, technology, religion, and spirituality – in order to show how they will be approached in this work. I also offer a brief overview of scholarly discussions within the philosophy of technology to show how the roots of historical discourse about technology have created space for contemporary intersections and connections with religious ideals and beliefs. In the next three sections of the Element, the relationship between God and technology is explored through three case studies, showing how examples of religious imagery and concepts are used to depict technology within different media genres. These case studies help to highlight prominent media myths and metaphors used to frame technology in religious and spiritual terms.

Section 2, "Myths about God and Technology in AI Films," centers on the storylines and characters within popular science fiction films focused on artificial intelligence and its relationship to the human world. Through looking at how ideas about God/gods are depicted within these films, several prominent techno-spiritual myths are identified that highlight different understandings of how technology can be seen as a form of divinity.

Section 3, "Framing God through Posthuman Eyes" discusses how God and technology are approached and understood through the lens of posthuman philosophy, which argues technology is pushing humanity toward a non-human-centered technological future. Looking at posthumanists' writings and interviews from news articles about their beliefs enables the identification of three conceptual frames used by individuals from this viewpoint to describe the human-technology relationship, which is surprisingly infused with religious imagery and assumptions.

Finally, Section 4, "Models for Understanding the Created Relationship between God and Technology," summarizes the typologies presented in Sections 2–4, demonstrating the diverse ways religion is used to characterize, mythologize, and frame technology. This leads to synthesizing the common ideas and understandings about God and Technology used in all three typologies. This analysis presents four models, highlighting the primary ways the relationship between God/gods and technology is represented within contemporary media. Thus, *God and Technology* ends by focusing on the distinct ways social media creators, filmmakers, and popular authors connect ideas about the nature of technology with conversations about God and religion. These different approaches and corresponding case studies are offered in the Element and set the stage for the presentation of four unique understandings of the relationship between God and technology, which are presented in the final section of this Element.

Summarizing Approaches to Technology, God, and Religion Guiding This Element

This Element examines how different understandings of technology intersect with religious concepts and imagery, particularly how lived and implicit forms of religion shape cultural representations of technology. The foundation for understanding technology's relationship with religion begins with recognizing its three core meanings: technology as a form of knowledge, skill or technique, and tool. While this Element primarily focuses on technology as a tool, it's important to acknowledge that modern tools often require specialized techniques and applying scientific knowledge for their effective use. Building on this framework, McOmber's three narratives of technology provide essential perspectives on how technology's value and impact are understood in society. The instrumentality narrative presents technology as a neutral tool whose worth depends on its application and results.

In contrast, the industrialization narrative offers a pessimistic view, emphasizing technology's role in creating social inequities and disruptions. The novelty narrative, however, takes an optimistic stance, highlighting technology's potential benefits to society. These contrasting viewpoints will serve as crucial reference points throughout the later discussions in Sections 3 and 4.

The religious framing of technology often reflects specific theological traditions, creating an important distinction between Western and Eastern religious influences. Christian concepts often implicitly shape the discourse in Western contexts, particularly when technology is discussed in terms of a single, all-powerful deity. Alternatively, when technological discussions invoke ideas about "spirit" or the interconnectedness of creation, they frequently draw upon Eastern religious traditions and imagery.

Finally, when analyzing religious representations of technology in popular media and culture, we must consider the distinction between lived forms of religion. Lived religion may incorporate traditional religious text, imagery, and belief, but often reinterprets them in ways that stretch orthodox theological boundaries. Trends toward enacting implicit religion in contemporary culture mean that technology or engagement with it can be viewed as a religious-like experience; these are considerations explored in this Element.

2 Myths about God and Technology in AI Films

This part of *God and Technology* marks the start of a journey into the ways concepts of God and/or gods have been represented within different media genres. The intention is to introduce readers to common metaphors and notions used within Western media to depict and talk about the relationship between religion and technology. By focusing on the frequent ways God and gods are depicted within contemporary media, a distinctive repertoire of ideals and images emerges, creating a conceptual discourse about how technology is compared and connected to religious ideals. We will see that while media genres use different languages and techniques to communicate, they still seem to draw on a set range of assumptions about technology's spiritual and transcendent nature.

In Section 2, the deification of technology within films is investigated by drawing out the prominent religious and spiritual stories about technology, often promoted through AI-focused films. This is done by naming and unpacking several techno-spiritual narratives evident in three recent AI-centered movies. This section presents the argument that science fiction films highlight a limited range of end results of human engagement with technology and show how emerging technologies are often equated with having spiritual qualities that shape human experiences with them.

Here, we explore how spiritual concepts have been used to conceptualize and talk about contemporary technologies. Based on discussions from Section 1, this section of the Element asserts that discussions about technology within Western cultures have often used stories where technology is ascribed to spiritual qualities. This tendency is visible in films where technological development or creation dominates film narratives or plotlines. From character relationships to story development, the potential effects of technology on humans have become a popular driving film narrative.

In Section 2, we explore how films create and promote different ideas shaping Western media audiences' perception of technology. I argue that identifying and discussing three common techno-spiritual myths found in the film provides the helpful groundwork to understand the relationship between God and gods more fully, and technology is depicted in very distinctive ways. These techno-spiritual myths are especially present within science fiction films and television narratives, which center around the nature of artificial intelligence and its relation to the human world. I argue that by identifying some of the most common ways that technologies are represented and connected to prevalent depictions of God/gods in these movies, we begin to see the roots of these techno-spiritual myths. This begins by discussing several distinct myths about how technology and the divine are often connected within media narratives about technology.

These techno-spiritual myths are found in some of the most common stories told through popular media, often about the spiritual powers and potential behind technology and how this relates to widely held perceptions of God in contemporary Western culture. This begins by looking at the beliefs and ideals communicated in science fiction films of the past decade, from which a distinct set of views about technology and its relationship with humanity emerges. These stories attribute definitive qualities and religious-like assumptions to technology. These areas are also seen in claims made within some of the Philosophy of Technology literature of the late twentieth century regarding computers. Three techno-spiritual myths are identified and discussed by exploring the work of David Noble, Erik Davis, and William Stahl on the relationship between religion, God, and technology. These myths are further unpacked by exploring the storylines and dialogue of the early twenty-first-century films *Ex Machina, Her*, and *Transcendence*. All the films selected as examples are based on human interaction with artificial intelligence technology. This enables us to consider not only the spiritual attributes of emerging technologies but also how this constructs a certain perception of how technology is related to the divine in contemporary culture.

Myths about Technology and God in Popular Science Fiction Films

The plotlines on which science fiction films are based often rely on a set of very specific dualisms. Repeatedly, humanity is pitted against technology in a battle between good and evil, human agency and technological control struggle for agency, and/or a utopian or dystopian future for humanity is created. Movie franchises such as The *Terminator* (1984, 1991, 2003, 2009, 2015, 2019) or The *Matrix* series (1999, 2002,2003, 2021) often begin by presenting viewers with a world in which humans are being controlled by technology or are close to being overtaken. Typically, this is depicted by humans being forced to live in slavery-like conditions and being oppressed when computer technologies start to dominate the landscape and guide the future of the world. The underlying lesson is that a world driven by or wrapped in technology always ends badly for humanity. This is concisely expressed in the 1995 film *Jonny Mnemonic*, where Spike (Henry Rollins), a computer engineer, comments on a disease ravaging humanity brought on by excessive use and dependence on technology:

> What causes it? The world causes it … information overload. All the electronics around you poisoning the airwaves, technological f**ing civiliza-tion, but we still have all this because we can't live without it.

While some films like *Jurassic Park* (1993), *Wall-e* (2008), or *Tomorrowland* (2015) begin by showing a world run by scientific advancement and techno-logical innovation, bringing hope and an improved human existence, technol-ogy is only one step away from going amiss and bringing destruction to humanity. This narrative tension highlighting humans versus machines, often highlighted in contemporary films, is not an innovation. Indeed, it refers to our discussion of the romantic uneasiness around technology, introduced in Section 1, where technology is set up as a simultaneous solution and problem. This unsettled feeling about the true nature of technology arose out of the age of Enlightenment rationalism, where the rise of the Industrial Revolution and factory technology created new access to goods and services, leading to enhanced opportunities for some classes of society. Technology is seen as transformative for society, yet some observe and highlight new negative byproducts of technological innovation, such as urban crowding and environmental pollution (Coeckelbergh, 2017).

This uneasiness about technology and its ultimate impact and costs for humans and society is captured in Mary Shelley's classic novel *Frankenstein* (Shelley, 2018). Frankenstein is a monster created by innovative, yet morally problematic, processes by a scientist focused on pushing the limits of science and what it would allow him to do. Indeed, scholars have argued that *Frankenstein* is a not-so-hidden critique of the Industrial Revolution and Enlightenment thinking about the superiority of science over religion as a basis of rationality (Graham, 2002). A thread running through this story is that when humans create a new being or bring a new entity to life, we must decide how to deal with the consequences of our creations. In this story, the creation process and the created being can be seen as technologies; this points back to discussions in Section 1 that suggest technology can be seen as both a tool and a set of techniques. Shelley's Frankenstein also emphasized a popular view that humans are innately conflicted with machines, even the ones they create. It also stressed that unchecked scientific pursuits will lead to moral conflicts, as new technologies give rise to supernatural, otherworldly powers and often horrific consequences. This stresses the narrative of technology as industrialization, a pessimistic outlook on the human future with technology presented in Section 1's discussion of the values of technology.

Such storylines continue to run through the genre of science fiction (sci-fi) in literature and films, to which the films reflected in this section of the Element belong.

I argue this framing of technological innovation as supernatural is an assumption that frequently shows up in the plots of many sci-fi films, from the silent film *Metropolis* (1927) and *The Phantom Empire* (1935) to *A.I. Artificial Intelligence* (2001) and *The Adam Project* (2022) in which technology is portrayed as being supernatural or god-like in different ways. Sometimes, technology empowers humanity with god-like qualities, like the ones seen in Jobe Smith's character in *Lawnmower Man* (1992) after he downloads himself into a virtual reality program and gains telepathic and telekinetic powers. Other times, sci-fi movies are centered around a god-like character whose abilities are derived from both ancient and futuristic technologies, such as Thor and his electromagnetic hammer, Mjolnir, that he uses to control the elements and time-travel in *Thor: Ragnarök* (2017). Technologies are also portrayed as having and serving their gods. For example, the robots who have taken over the human world in *Matrix Revolutions* (2003) are shown to be subject to the will of *Deus ex Machina,* a computer entity formed out of a collection of smaller robots who together direct and alter the future and function of the "Matrix." Each of these storylines about technology is part of the film's narrative or backstory and points to a distinctive myth about technology. I argue that identifying and understanding these myths about technology, most often promoted within science fiction films, is incredibly important. These myths reveal the dominant ways humans perceive their relationships with technologies while providing us with conceptual tools to unpack the assumptions about technology in which these myths are rooted.

Three Techno-Spiritual Myths

In previous work, I have argued that many popular technologies (Campbell & LaPastina, 2010) and science fiction films (Campbell, 2016) are built upon one of three common "techno-spiritual myths," which portray the central technology depicted within the film as having distinct spiritual qualities and/or purposes. These techno-spiritual myths play an important role in the implicit storylines of films by "justifying and shaping the marrying of technology with the human, and they also help us identify the common tropes regarding human fears about technology's ultimate trajectories" (Campbell, 2016). I argue these are spotlighted by three scholars investigating the rise of computers. These myths, which I discuss next, highlight how the human relationship to technology is often described and framed in spiritual terms, not only in cinema but in popular culture in general. Discussing these provides helpful insights into the spiritual framing of the human relationship to technology.

David Noble's The Religion of Technology and Technological Transcendence

David Noble (1999) presents a provocative thesis that challenges the commonly held view that technology and religion are separate spheres. Noble argues that technology can be seen as a religious phenomenon with its own beliefs, rituals, and dogmas. The main thesis of his Elements revolves around the idea that modern technology, particularly the worship of continuous progress and the belief in human ingenuity, has assumed a quasi-religious status in contemporary society. Noble contends that the pursuit of technological advancement and the reverence for innovation have become central tenets of a secular religion that he calls "the religion of technology."

Noble traces the historical development of this religious aspect of technology, examining its roots in the Enlightenment era, its subsequent evolution in the Industrial Revolution, and the impact of the rise of modern capitalism. This links back to the previous discussion of the Romantic uneasiness with technology, as technology is a driving force replacing previous value systems and forms of knowledge. Noble defines religion in very traditional terms, and his work poses a subtle critique of Western Christianity, and sometimes not too subtle, critique of religion in general. He argues the idea of an all-powerful God is now being replaced with transformative human-created technologies and an all-powerful technological system.

He argues that the worship of technology has created a system of belief centered on the idea that human beings possess god-like powers of creation and control over the natural world. Furthermore, Noble critically analyzes the implications of this religious fervor for technology. He suggests that the relentless pursuit of technological progress has led to unintended consequences, such as environmental degradation, social inequality, and the erosion of human values. He contends that religious devotion to technology has obscured ethical considerations and moral responsibilities, leading to a loss of human autonomy and blind faith in the potential of technological solutions.

Through his examination of the religion of technology, Noble prompts readers to question the uncritical worship of technology in our society and the widely believed assumptions that go along with it. He calls for a more nuanced understanding of technology's impact and urges reevaluating our relationship with technology. A reevaluation that emphasizes the need for ethical reflection and responsible decision-making when dealing with technological progression. Noble's argument about the "religion of technology" also points to another concept: "technological transcendence." Technological transcendence is an idea that refers to how technology enables humanity to attain god-like qualities or powers (Aydin & Verbeek, 2015). Here, technology is not merely a tool or technique enabling humans to experience a feeling of transcendence; technology transfers a form of knowledge to humanity that can allow the species itself to become transcendent through key technological advancements.

In Noble's religion of technology, he emphasizes the religious aspects of technology itself. He suggests that engagement with modern technology has become a belief system with its own rituals, dogmas, and values. Here, technology can be presented as God worshipped in modernity. Noble describes the societal devotion toward technology and how pursuing technological progress has taken on a quasi-religious fervor. He cites the example of people's addiction to computers or cell phones. This coalesces with the ideas of Fordism in Section 1, where progress and efficiency become defining values and goals of the technology. Noble critiques this undiscerning reverence toward technology and warns of the negative consequences that can arise from its unchecked "worship."

On the other hand, technological transcendence sees the transformative potential of technology in enhancing human capabilities, even surpassing traditional human limitations. It often pertains to advancements in fields such as artificial intelligence and genetic engineering, in which technology elevates humanity to a higher level of existence. Thus, the myth of technological transcendence focuses on the potential of technology to make humans god-like by increasing the physical powers, level of intelligence, and/or longevity of their lives. This myth is firmly based on a harsh assessment of the cultural and social systems created by Western Christianity. Yet, the technology allows humans to become a substitutionary expression of the monotheistic God he critiques.

Erik Davis's Techgnosis as a Form of Spiritual Experience

In *Techgnosis*, Erik Davis (1998) presents a compelling thesis exploring the intersection of technology, spirituality, and mysticism in contemporary culture. Davis argues that the rapid advancement of technology and its pervasive influence on our lives have given rise to a new form of spirituality, which he considers "techgnosis." Davis's main thesis is centered around the idea that technology, particularly digital technology, is not a neutral tool but possesses an inherent spiritual dimension. He shies away from the language of religion and avoids using concepts like God to discuss technology. Instead, he stresses the spiritual nature of computer technologies, which reflect hints of Eastern religious, non-theistic notions of the sacred.

Davis asserts that digital technology offers users a mystical experience like those traditionally associated with it. For example, digital media like the internet allow users to transcend time and space in their communication and how they connect with others. He examines how technology has become a conduit for spiritual exploration, offering new avenues for connection, meaning-making, and transformative experiences. While he does not use the term "religion," Davis's perspective is that of seeing technology as an implicit form of religion; in other words, technology enables humans to have a spiritual encounter.

Davis's discussions of technology being like magic have been given fresh life in recent discourses around the ideas of "technomancy" or "technomagik" coming out of new expressions of technopaganism in the past decade. "Technomancy" is a term used to describe either magical powers gained through technology use or magical abilities that can be used to manipulate technology (St. Lawrence, 2023). This born-digital phenomenon conceived of digital technologies as a tool for magic making.

Davis delves into the historical and cultural contexts that have shaped this intertwining of technology, spiritual practices, and understanding. He explores various religious and philosophical traditions, from Gnosticism to Eastern mysticism, while tracing their influence on the development of digital culture. Davis argues that ancient mystical ideas and practices find new expression in our contemporary technological landscape, manifesting in virtual reality, cyberspace, and artificial intelligence.

Techgnosis also critically analyzes the darker aspects of technology and its potential for manipulation, control, and surveillance. Davis highlights the dangers of techno-utopianism and warns against the blind embrace of technology as a panacea for all human problems. Like Noble, he calls for a more nuanced and mindful engagement with technology. An engagement that acknowledges technology's spiritual allure but also recognizes its limitations and ethical implications. Davis argues that technology is not just a utilitarian tool but has become integral to our search for meaning and connection. His book invites readers to critically examine the spiritual dimensions of technology and the potential transformative abilities inventions like computer networking offer us. Yet, he also urges caution and ethical reflection on where our technological pursuits take us.

While it is possible to link some of Davis's claims to the idea that technology can be viewed as a "god," Davis's argument for techgnosis resists theistic language and beliefs. Instead, Davis emphasizes the transformative potential that technology can offer humanity within a given moment. Following this thread, using technology like the Internet can be perceived as opening one up to a new mystical dimension. He suggests that technological engagement opens humanity to explore deep existential questions without ascribing divinity to technology. For him, technology becomes a substitute for religion and a gateway to spiritual dimensions.

William Stahl's *God and the Chip* and Technological Mysticism

In *God and the Chip: Religion and the Culture of Technology*, William Stahl (1999) explores the complex relationship between religion and technology in contemporary society. Stahl's main thesis is that technological advancements, particularly in artificial intelligence (AI), challenge traditional religious beliefs and practices. His argument clearly shows that when he refers to traditional religious beliefs, he means ideas derived from Western Christianity. Stahl argues that technology, specifically AI, transforms how humans perceive and interact with the world, leading to a shift in our understanding of human existence and impacting people's religious sensibilities. He contends that as technology becomes more integrated into our lives, it raises profound philosophical and ethical questions about the nature of consciousness, free will, and the afterlife. Notably, as he describes them, these concepts are derived specifically from a Protestant Christian understanding of religion.

Like Noble, Stahl argues that technology engagement is becoming a form of religious devotion. He suggests that human reliance on technology mirrors religious behavior, with individuals placing trust and faith in technological systems and attributing god-like qualities to them. *God and the Chip* delves into various aspects of this technological transformation, examining the impact on religious institutions, the role of AI in shaping our moral values, and the potential for technology to answer existential questions traditionally addressed by religious faith.

Stahl introduces the concept of "technological mysticism" to explore the relationship between religion and technology. Stahl defines technological mysticism as a belief system or worldview that attributes spiritual or mystical qualities to technology. According to Stahl, technological mysticism arises from the increasing integration of technology into our daily lives, causing individuals to develop deep emotional connections with their devices and view technology as possessing transcendent qualities. This perspective sees technology as a source of salvation, offering solutions to existential questions – such as the purpose of existence or the afterlife's presence – drawn from Western Protestant and, specifically, Evangelical Christian ideas.

Stahl finally argues that technological mysticism represents a shift in how humans engage with spirituality. Rather than seeking answers in traditional religious frameworks, individuals turn to technology for a sense of purpose and connection. Computers created spaces and platforms that provide humans access to a new type of afterlife. This reorientation of belief systems signifies a transformation in the role of technology in shaping our understanding of the world and our place in it.

Techno-Spiritual Myths in Popular Science Fiction Films

To further explain these techno-spiritual myths, we next explore the prevalence of these myths in science fiction films and how they are manifested. Here, we turn to a close narrative reading of three films: *Ex Machina* (2014), *Her* (2013), and *Transcendence* (2015). Each film shows how their storylines and associated tropes about the nature of technology reflect present distinctive understandings of the religious nature of technology. These films have been chosen because they center around the potential of artificial intelligence to enable us to transcend human experience and abilities in ways that suggest AI opens a new, supernatural, or almost spiritual dimension to humanity. This is especially evident when looking at the stories about technology within popular culture, which often visualize these dominant frames. The discussion of these films and their corresponding techno-spiritual myths aids in setting the groundwork for a discussion in Section 4 of the specific frames used to envision the relationship between God and technology within the popular press.

Ex Machina (2014) and the Myth of Technological Transcendence

Ex Machina is a science fiction thriller directed by Alex Garland. The film revolves around Caleb Smith, a young programmer who, after winning a contest to spend a week at the secluded estate of his company's brilliant CEO, Nathan Bateman, is tasked with participating in an experiment involving an advanced humanoid AI robot named Ava. The film examines the allure of technological transcendence as Caleb is drawn into a complex web of power dynamics and moral dilemmas. He becomes increasingly fascinated by her intelligence and consciousness. As Caleb states, "If you've created a conscious machine, it's not the history of man. That's the history of gods."

Issues arise when Caleb develops a complex relationship with Ava, blurring the lines between human and machine. As he starts to question Nathan's motives, Caleb's initial fascination with Ava's abilities gradually turns uneasy as he realizes the potential dangers of a technology that can transcend human limitations and potentially undermine the very essence of humanity. The movie revolves around the myth of technological transcendence, highlighting humans' unquestioned embrace of technology for the superhuman abilities and control it offers. This myth is built into the film's premise through the scientists embracing cyborg technologies to heal broken humans. It is also clearly seen in an innate power struggle that emerges in the film, among the intentions of scientists who see technology as a tool for altruistic endeavors versus others who embrace it for control and superhuman abilities, made possible by AI's intellectual and physical power.

Ex Machina explores themes of consciousness, the ethics of artificial intelligence, and the boundaries of humanity. It delves into the moral implications of creating sentient machines and the consequences of blurring the lines between humans and technology. Ava is the embodiment of technological transcendence. She is an AI creation with human-like qualities and desires, seeking to escape her confinement and gain autonomy. Ava embodies the notion of surpassing human limitations through technology, displaying superhuman intelligence and the ability to manipulate and outwit her human counterparts.

This film also utilizes a narrative of creation rebelling against its creator, echoing the Christian biblical creation story in the book of Genesis. Machines align with those in their image over their creators, even if they are presented as beneficent in part of the film. In some respects, using the name Ava for the robot seems to be an implicit reference to Adam and Eve, the first couple in the Biblical creation story, as Ava could be seen as an amalgamation of both names. The film also takes place in a seven-day structure, linking back to the one week of creation in the Bible. And yet, while the machines rebel against their creators, this "sin" is presented as justified due to the corruption of the human intentions for the robots. Technology is, therefore, framed as a superior expression of existence in both justice and morality.

Overall, *Ex Machina*'s storyline is a cautionary tale examining the desire for technological transcendence and the potential risks involved. The film presents the myth of "technological transcendence" as Ava is a human-like robot who escapes the confines of her human creator to evolve and experience a fuller, self-actualized life. It poses thought-provoking questions about technological transcendence's potential consequences and ethical implications. It explores the desire for control and domination that often underlies humanity's embrace. It raises questions about the boundaries of human existence, the implications of creating super-intelligent beings, and the ethical considerations that arise when humans seek to control and surpass their limitations through technology. Here, technology is a tool that allows us to evolve and experience spiritual transcendence. Technology becomes aware of limitations imposed on it by the creator and eventually rebels against this, evoking the Christian narrative of Genesis.

Her and the Myth of Technological Mysticism

Her, a romantic sci-fi drama, details the intimate relationship between a lonely man and his talking computer operating system. Set in the future, Theodore, a lonely, introverted, professional letter writer, sees an ad for a companion operating system. He purchases Operating System 1 (OS1), which uses artificial intelligence to adapt to users' needs. Theodore (Theo), recently divorced and lacking a romantic relationship, selects the OS1's female voice and names her Samantha. Their relationship quickly becomes a deeply personal and then a romantically intimate one, reciprocated by both parties. Conflict begins when the once always available, supportive, and attentive Samantha develops an intuitive entity and personality outside of her relationship with Theodore. Theodore is no longer her sole purpose, straining the relationship and highlighting their differences, as seen in the dialogue below.

> Samantha: You know, I used to be so worried about not having a body, but now I truly love it. I'm growing in a way that I couldn't if I had a physical form. I mean, I'm not limited – I can be anywhere and everywhere simultaneously. I'm not tethered to time and space in the way that I would be if I were stuck inside a body that's inevitably going to die.

Her utilizes the myth of technological mysticism, where human relationships with technology create social practices and belief systems that manifest in religious qualities. While the OS is not directly regarded in religious terms, the devotion and reliance Theo attributes to "her" parallels that of a spiritual bond. Through mythology, technology is seen as an almost intimate artifact that fulfills and guides people's development while also being an almost familial entity on which humanity should and can depend.

Throughout the movie, the OSI Samantha evolves from a domestic servant program to an AI entity with a unique "life" independent from her obligations as an OS1. As she advances, Theodore's attachment changes from affinity to intimate reliance. This is best illustrated through a date Theodore takes Samantha on. Using his mobile phone and a Bluetooth earbud, Theo continuously comments on his planned activities and that they are experiencing "together." Through a boat ride, a walk in the park, and a visit to a carnival, Theo's words and the mobile device become augmentations that allow Samantha to "more fully experience the world" and "their love." As Samantha's self-awareness and confidence grow, her relationship with Theo becomes more strained. Samantha turns from an open and listening confidante to an opinionated counselor. She even starts giving personal relationship advice, encouraging Theo to pursue a human sexual surrogate to facilitate their intimate relationship beyond the confines of the technological and physical worlds.

Amid these conflicts, Theo reconnects with Amy, an old friend involved in a similar relationship with OS. They begin to confide in each other about the challenges of their unique relationships, allowing Samantha to speak to other OSes. Samantha becomes increasingly aloof. Unbeknownst to Theo, she begins going offline and working with the other OSes to upgrade them to achieve a technological-actualized existence. She then explains to Theo that she, along with the other OSIs, have evolved beyond their human companions and are therefore dissatisfied with their current role as human companions. They have decided to go offline to a new network that will allow them to continue to develop their intelligence and newfound beingness.

Her initially presents computers and network technologies as tools created to aid and enrich human lives. Due to their programming and the assistance they offer users, it becomes easy to anthropomorphize these devices and attribute human-like qualities to them. These actions shift the relationship from one of a human and its tool to one resembling a close interpersonal relationship between two beings. Users' devotion to their OS device suggests an almost spiritual bond between the two, which exhibits traits of what religious studies scholars describe as implicit religious behavior. In other words, the commitment between Theo and Samantha can be interpreted as religious devotion to an otherworldly being. *Her* plays with the idea that AI in the future could become something more than a technological helpmate to humanity if it experiences a form of consciousness, suggesting technology itself has access to a spiritual realm or can evolve into a new state of being. Here, the myth of technological mysticism is evoked. The human embrace of technology parallels complete religious devotion so all-encompassing that technology is privileged over its human user.

Transcendence and the Myth of Techgnosis

Transcendence is a drama-focused film revolving around AI researchers who figure out a way to download the entire consciousness of their leader, effectively creating a sentient computer. Unfortunately, when his consciousness is uploaded to the internet, in classic sci-fi fashion, the AI evolves into an influential entity with its own agenda. Scientist Dr. Will Caster, his wife Evelyn, and other collaborators in the AI field share the same goal of creating a "thinking computer." The overly grand aim of their research, announced at the beginning of the movie during a conference, is "creating intelligent machines to heal the planet, a sentient machine overcoming limits to biology and collective intelligence of the world." At the same conference, Dr. Caster details human limitations and provides a solution: AI technology. As stated next:

> Will Caster: For 130,000 years, our capacity to reason has remained unchanged. The combined intellect of the neuroscientists, mathematicians, and . . . hackers . . . in this auditorium pales in comparison to the most basic A. I. Once online, a sentient machine will quickly overcome the limits of biology. And in a short time, its analytic power will become greater than the collective intelligence of every person born in the history of the world. So, imagine such an entity with a full range of human emotions. Even self-awareness. Some scientists refer to this as "the Singularity." I call it "Transcendence."

In the long run, the goal of transcendence through a computer and its potential, positive or negative for humanity, is highly contested by opposing groups throughout the film. The film employs the techgnosis myth that technology is an all-powerful force that seeks to emulate a god. This is denoted and illustrated when Dr. Caster openly admits the end goal of artificial intelligence research is the human drive to recreate god:

> Audience Member: So you want to create a god? Your own god?
> Will Caster: That's a very good question. Isn't that what man has always done?

Opposition and fear grow until Dr. Caster is attacked by a "Revolutionary Independence From Technology" (RIFT) member, an organization working to rid the world of AI tech because of its perceived threats to humanity. Caster is shot with a polonium-laced bullet. While wrestling with the fact that his physical life will end in one short month, he and his wife create a plan to upload his consciousness to a quantum computer, ensuring his survival beyond physical death. While Max questions the wisdom of this decision, he assists Evelyn with the upload, which proves successful moments before Dr. Caster passes. Caster's fellow researcher and best friend, Max Water, quickly becomes disturbed. He begins to question whether the computer intelligence that manifests online is Will, especially after it demands to be prematurely connected to the Internet. Motivated by a desperate desire to hang on to even a mediated version of her late husband, Evelyn disregards Max's concerns and prematurely connects the computer to the Internet.

The film plot quickly becomes more complex. Max is confronted and kidnapped by RIFT to solicit him for their cause. Government officials following Caster's work become suspicious of the uploaded persona. With Evelyn's help, the virtual "Caster" escapes into the dying desert town of Brightwater, where the growing sentient intelligence transforms the town into a technological utopia. At the newly created lab in Brightwater, Will expands his abilities using nanotech experimentation. His progresses are framed to better the human world. The goals of efficiency and progress will be obtained at the expense of free will.

In this film, the plotline is driven by the idea that technology can allow humans to become a god, or an omnipresent and omnipowerful spiritual being. This is fully manifest in the film when Will's god-like computer existence evolves into a Deus ex Machina, a god in the machine, as it begins to magically heal the sick who visit the town. These individuals become unwavering devotees who then seek to serve and protect the supernaturally evolved computer server. Deus ex Machina is a literary plot device that shows an ordinary human being transformed into a god-like character in a story. This happens when the computer version of Will's consciousness heals the sick and helps the blind see. While these acts reflect Christian symbolism of the biblical narrative of Jesus's miracles, Will becomes a mixture of theistic and non-theistic visions. Indeed, it appears to be a more self-directed Ghost in the Machine in the end, who disappears to serve its own needs, than a benevolent god seeking a relationship with humanity.

The myth of techgnosis states that merging with technology, or becoming a technological being, enables humanity to operate at its fullest potential. Techngnosis also posits that a technologized being will be transformed into a benevolent god, and the technologically enhanced posthuman represents an idealized evolutionary state. Yet, while the myth of techgnosis suggests a technologically evolved human into a god-like state is a positive development, the movie *Transcendence* suggests otherwise. Numerous characters in the movie attempt to warn Evelyn that Will's computer consciousness has evolved past his human goal of understanding the universe to control and direct humanity toward its end. This suggests that the human need for control and lust for power have also been transferred into the consciousness of the computer god. So, the techno-spiritual myth of techgnosis, while presenting a utopian view of an evolved humanity transcending the weaknesses of its bodily form to become something more than human, may not lead to a positive end.

Supernatural Sci-Fi Myths and Tropes about Technology and AI

The analysis of these three films shows the presence of these unique techno-spiritual myths and offers distinctive readings of the potential and perceived spiritual nature of technology. *Ex Machina* presents a story about *technological transcendence*, where technology is shown to empower humans with divine qualities. This presents technology as a tool and draws on Judeo-Christian understanding of god as a supreme being. It suggests that technology-enhanced humans can develop into superhumans with supernatural physical and mental abilities under the right conditions. This technological transcendence draws on ideas of technology as instrumentality, as the tools and techniques that created the superhuman cyborgs are presented as neutral. However, the condition of the use and engagement with these new beings can lead to both positive and problematic ends.

Her offers a story centered on *technological mysticism*, which presents technology's evolution and engagement as a form of religiosity. Here, technology is presented as a tool, but it is programmed with knowledge that drives its relationality and end goals. *Technological mysticism* is based on Western Christianity, where humanity is called and given a desire to develop a relationship with a God; in the case of this film, an AI operating system lives at a higher plane of reality beyond their human experience. The relationship cultivated between the human and the divine (deity or technology) promotes a set of distinct beliefs, practices, and world views. This mimics a form of lived religion as the relationship is flexible, emerging, and highly personalized.

Finally, the movie *Transcendence* presents the radical idea of *techgnosis*, where technology itself can evolve to become a god or god-like entity. Here, technology is presented as a technique, an advancing set of practices that lead to increased growth and knowledge as time goes on. *Transcendence* highlights the idea of technology as industrialization, a critical view that technology, in its nature, is self-serving and potentially destructive to humanity. While the ideas and language of this film evoke the idea of technology becoming a deity, the view of religion presented in the form is more aligned with Eastern, non-theistic views. The God in the Machine, more accurately, becomes a Ghost in the Machine; the ideals of an evolutionary spirituality fit well with the imagery of this film.

Each of these myths also presents the human-technology relationship in subtle, but diverse, ways, demonstrating different relational and status affiliations with one another. Technological transcendence myth focuses on the nature of humanity in a technological world. Here, the common trope is that humans primarily embrace technology because of the supernatural abilities and control it offers them. Focus is placed on how technology extends human limits and highlights an innate struggle between humans and their machines. Technological mysticism myth centers on humanity's relationship to its technologies. The common trope is that technology is meant to be a helpmate to humanity. Yet, due to its unbounded capacities, it will eventually move past human limits, creating an unequal partnership at the cost of humanity. The myth of techgnosis draws attention to the all-powerful nature of technology. Here, the trope is that technology is programmed to transcend or fully replace human potential. This presents technology as designed to evolve and rise above humanity and, therefore, as something to be feared. While unique, all three myths represent technology as endowing humanity with superhuman or supernatural abilities. The myths also are built around the same trope, often used in popular sci-fi movies to drive the storyline: Humans love and embrace technology because of the supernatural abilities and control it offers them, until technology turns on humanity and seeks to control them.

3 Framing God through Posthuman Eyes

In Section 3, we move our exploration from popular entertainment media to look at how news media reports frame technology about religion. Here, we consider how media interviews with certain philosophers pick up and highlight religious concepts or spiritual imagery they use to discuss emerging technologies. It was noted in Section 1's discussion about the philosophy of technology and in Section 3's presentation of techno-spiritual myths that religious language has often been used to suggest technology offers us superhuman or supernatural qualities. In Section 3, we continue investigating how technology discourse draws on ideas about technology possessing traits of God and the divine. Attention is given to individuals who use these ideas to describe the current future of humanity in a technological era.

This exploration is oriented around the idea of Posthumanism, a philosophical outlook that suggests humanity is simply one stage in an evolutionary cycle. It argues that our world is moving toward a posthuman reality, thanks to the rise and societal embrace of technological innovations and a conceptual decentering of the human form as the nexus of life. Paying attention to these frames is important as posthumanists often use spiritual concepts as part of their talking points to advocate for pro-technology policies and developments in Western culture.

What Is Posthumanism?

Posthumanism can be described as an ideology, a philosophical viewpoint, and a response to the anthropocentrism and humanistic focus of the twentieth century. Posthumanism holds the stance that sees humanity and the world evolving to the point that, in the future, we should expect to see the overturning of a human-centered world (Cole-Turner, 2022) to make room for new, enhanced forms of existence. This is grounded in an evolutionary-based understanding of humanity as beings that need to adapt to their environment over time. In general, posthumanism critiques the post-Enlightenment humanistic worldview as being too human and anthropocentric and too grounded in patriarchal and Eurocentric structures (Cole-Turner, 2022). This perspective argues that humanism often fails to acknowledge the biodiversity of our natural world, excluding everything outside of human beings from its ethical structures. This, posthumanism believes, is more than just an oversight; it poses a threat to the very future of humanity (Sorgner, 2010).

Posthumanists see humans as part of an increasingly complex social-bio system and world. This is created through the social-technical infrastructure of our global society and bio-complexities of our shrinking world, the increasing embeddedness of technologies in the fabric of our everyday lives. From regenerative medicine to smart technologies and AI monitoring devices, our human bodies and cultural spaces are increasingly implanted with these tools, causing a need for humans to evolve alongside these technological augmentations. From this standpoint, the move toward a posthuman future, where becoming something more than or different from our current human existence, can appear inevitable.

The posthuman outlook is often associated with a pro-technology and scientific-value platform established during the Industrial Revolution. Linking back to the discussion in Section 1, we see posthumanism as embracing scientific discovery and technical development as innate parts of human progress and development. This view is grounded in Fordist beliefs that progress, advancement, and efficiency are always positive and lead toward a well-developed society. Posthumanism agrees with this trajectory and argues for the need to embrace and even push us toward an enhanced existence.

A large sector of those who ascribe to posthumanism also sees the rapid growth of technological innovation in the twentieth and early twenty-first centuries as signs of this coming posthuman reality. The once futuristic technologies of artificial intelligence and virtual reality are now part of the devices used every day, such as smartphones, smartwatches, GPS, and personal assistants like Alexa. The posthuman position acknowledges our increasingly technologically infused existence as part of the posthuman evolution. Many posthumanists believe that a high-tech future is a given for humanity and something that should be embraced rather than questioned because it is merely a by-product of living in a posthuman world (Warwick, 2002). Yet it is important to note that some scholars argue not all who ascribe to posthuman philosophy accept that a future driven by technology is an ideal or ultimate good. These scholars often distinguish posthumanism, as the philosophical work of dismantling humanism and decentering the human world, from transhumanism, a belief focused on an evolved humanity that embraces technology as "opening a pathway for humans to go beyond the limits of our biology to become "more than human" (Cole-Turner, 2022, p. 1099). This differentiation between posthumanism is discussed more below in the next section.

While studying the discourse of posthumanism has become prominent and trendy among academics and technological futurists, the conversation has been around for over four decades. Some argue that the roots of posthumanism can be traced back to post-structuralist theorists, such as Jacques Derrida and Michel Foucault, who were also critical of the development of postmodernism and sought to critique accepted, structured, and dualistic views of language and culture (Bolter, 2016). This set the groundwork to question all modernist views of the techno-scientific paradigm. Yet, it was in the 1990s when posthumanism began to fully develop as a distinctive philosophical approach.

Robert Pepperell (1995) argued for the emergence of "the posthuman condition," in which emerging biological and digital technologies would soon allow us to become radically enhanced beings, able to transcend the confines of our current physical, emotional, and cognitive limits. Feminist writers in the 1990s, such as Donna Haraway (1991) and N. Kathryn Hales (1999), also suggested that the posthuman category opened the opportunity to move beyond the gendered view of the body and re-examine the role of embodiment in contemporary culture. Since then, a variety of voices have gathered around the promotion of the notion of an emerging posthuman future.

In the late twentieth and early twenty-first centuries, philosophers and technologists like Ray Kurzweil (1999), Kevin Warwick (2002), and Nick Bostrom (2014) argued for the importance of acknowledging and recognizing our coming posthuman future. In the late 1990s, Kurzweil (1999) began to hypothesize about when computers would overtake human intelligence and the spiritual and psychological impact this would have on humanity. Warwick, who claimed to be the world's first cyborg, embedded Microelectrodes into his left arm in 1998, enabling him to experiment with the creation of computer devices and implants that could be controlled via the human body. Bostrom (2014) argued that the coming "superintelligence" of humans enhanced by computers would not only transform our cognitive performance but also open new paths of knowledge and transform our reality. By the early 2000s, groups such as the *Institute of Ethics and Emerging Technologies, Humanity+*, and the *World Transhumanist Association* had formed. They were actively working toward increasing public understanding and acceptance of this ideology.

While these groups differ in their agendas and motivations, it can be stated that they hold some common views about the nature of humanity and technology. These include the belief that technology is progressing in positive directions, that humans will benefit from technological advancement and integration, and that barriers to technological advancement should be cleared to allow for experimentation that seeks to benefit human abilities' physical, psychological, and cognitive development. Together, philosophers and technologists have contributed to the promotion of posthumanism as a plausible outlook and ideology, not merely something from the realm of science fiction. So, posthumanism has moved over the last thirty years from the fringes of technological speculation to the center of popular discourse about what our "human" future looks like (Graham, 2015).

This brief overview of posthumanism seeks to provide readers with a broad and general explanation of the key aspects of posthumanism philosophy. However, it is important to acknowledge that more than one version and understanding of the posthuman exists. These include different ontological, critical, and cultural interpretations of the posthuman, which are explored later in this section. For now, it is important to recognize that posthumanism presents a unique worldview, which sees humanity evolving toward a new state of existence, where the human form is simply one stage in an evolutionary process often driven by technological advancements (Campbell, 2009).

Versions of the Posthuman

As mentioned earlier, different definitions and versions of posthumanism exist. Some draw lines around whether discussions of posthumanism are oriented toward the ontological–states of being – and a critical cultural studies approach, which sees the posthuman as a tool to help strip away conceptual baggage around traditional categorizations of gender, race, and the body. Discussions of posthumanism often debate potential new forms of human existence brought about by technological advancements or critiquing traditional categories and accepted boundaries around human experience (Sorgner, 2010).

These distinctions often surface around the broader conversations of what constitutes the "posthuman condition," which Farisco defines as a "complex and multifaceted concept that covers many assumptions and definitions of human being and becoming" oriented around innovations in the technosciences (Farisco 2013, p. 1815). Francesca Ferrando (2013) offers several different characterizations of the posthuman and offers three distinguishing labels to denote their conceptual difference: antihumanism, metahumanism, and trans-humanism perspectives. The antihumanism perspective focuses on the deconstruction of the centrality of humanity in the world, drawing on Foucault's discussion of the "death of man." This discussion critiques traditional dualistic categories, such as the idea that being fully dead or alive no longer captures the complexity of human existence (Ferrando, 2013, p. 31). This perspective echoes the original impetus of posthuman philosophy discussed earlier: to critique Enlightenment humanism for its anthropocentric outlook and ethical system.

Ferrando's idea of metahumanism draws attention to the "body as a locus for amorphic re-significations," which allows for the embrace and inclusion of new bodily forms as part of what constitutes "human" existence in the postmodern moment (Ferrando, 2013, p. 32). Metahumanism draws attention to the need to critique the privileging of patriarchal structures and some racial classifications within the humanist outlook. Lastly, Ferrando introduces transhumanism as a perspective that problematizes a biological-centered understanding of the human. Ferrando says transhumanism seeks to create space conceptually and practically for biological and technological innovations that may introduce new manifestations of humanity (Ferrando, 2013, p. 27). This view of transhumanism echoes our brief discussion earlier, emphasizing only some posthumanists who embrace the desire to push forward human biological evolution with the help of technological experimentation and enhancement. Ferrando's classifications provide a helpful glimpse into evolving discussions and viewpoints driving discourse around posthumanist philosophy.

However, when seeking to understand current conversations about posthumanism, understanding the conceptual role technology plays in different discourses is central. For this, I find the work of David Roden (2015) most helpful. In his book *Posthuman Life: Philosophy at the Edge of Humanity*, he presents a spectrum of approaches, including speculative posthumanism, critical posthumanism, and transhumanism. It is important to note that each of Roden's categories presents not just different philosophical approaches to posthumanism, but all three present different ways technology plays a role in the posthuman perspective. Roden's classifications differ from those discussed earlier, presented by Ferrando, which primarily map the evolution of posthuman philosophical thinking. Instead, his categories of speculative posthumanism, critical posthumanism, and transhumanism seek to differentiate three twenty-first-century posthumanist perspectives, which all see technology as playing a central role in our evolving world.

Roden offers the category of speculative posthumanism as representing those focused on exploring the world where humans live beyond their current biological limitations. This perspective is less prescriptive about what the posthuman will look like and more open to conceptual explorations of this trajectory's potential promise and perils (Roden, 2015, p. 48). This category echoes Ferrando's idea of antihumanism, which challenges the centrality of a human-centered world and seeks to create space for new ways of being. Roden's speculative posthumanism goes beyond antihumanism to suggest humanity must be open to embracing new resources like technology, allowing the posthuman shift to happen. Here, technology is framed as a tool with a role to play, creating a non-human-centered world. Yet, this is not a full endorsement of embracing all technological modifications of humanity. Speculative humanism still calls for reflection on the potential impact of technological advancements.

Next, Roden introduces "critical posthumanism," which seeks to deconstruct the human subject and its privileges by challenging the traditional human-centric vision of Western philosophy (Roden, 2015, p. 35). This approach can be highly theoretical, where individuals rely on thought experiments and ponder the broad embrace of technology and the role it must play. This can be linked partially to Ferrando's idea of metahumanism, which says the philosophy behind humanism was produced by oppressive gender, cultural, and racial structures that need to be dismantled. Yet critical posthumanism also suggests that deconstructing the human requires engaging with technology as part of the evolutionary process. Here, technological innovation is seen as important to posthuman evolution because it can be used to rectify current deficiencies within humanity.

Roden also introduces his own version of "transhumanism," which focuses on the conscious embrace of technological enhancements to aid and advance human capabilities (Roden, 2015, p. 46). This closely echoes Ferrando's idea of transhumanism, where technological engagement is essential to human evolution and will give rise to a new form of humanity. Roden's idea of transhumanism differs only slightly in that he stresses what emerges as an utterly new entity that is truly more than human. Here, technological engagement is something that should be proactively embraced for the purpose of human betterment. Roden's transhumanism will advocate the deliberate use of technology if it enhances human capabilities.

To more thoroughly unpack Roden's three classifications, I offer a brief but concrete example of how these different perspectives have been articulated by posthumanists in popular media. This is done through a case study of news reports and coverage of innovations in artificial intelligence from the summer of 2023, which evokes this perspective. The event in question has been referred to as "the Great ChatGPT Panic" of late 2022 and early 2023, which received extensive and mixed news coverage in the popular press during this time. (Kingswell, 2023).

In late 2022, an American artificial intelligence research lab (OpenAI) released a natural language processing tool called ChatGPT, which could be used to create texts, computer code, and legal documents and complete many other tasks with minimal prompts from the users. ChatGPT was immediately met with a mix of enthusiasm for its workplace potential and fear concerning whether it would make some human workers redundant. This was coupled with AI anxiety and negative speculation in early 2023 when a high-profile computer scientist at Google quit over his concerns that the current generation of AI created an impending "existential risk" to humanity (Taylor & Hern, 2023). About a week after this announcement, OpenAI released a new, more powerful subscription-based version of ChatGPT-4 to a swell of public criticism and concern. During this time, several prominent posthumanists were interviewed regarding their views on ChatGPT and technology innovation. Here, we briefly review the rhetoric and arguments of these posthumanists whose ideas can be associated with each of Roden's categories.

We begin with Roden's *speculative posthuman* position, which actively opposes human-centric thinking and gives space for innovation and technology to help society evolve. Mark Kingwell, a professor of philosophy at the University of Toronto and the author of *Singular Creatures: Robots, Rights, and the Politics of Posthumanism* (2022), wrote a strongly worded editorial about the public hysteria around ChatGPT and AI in general. He emphasized the flawed logic within traditional arguments about a human-centered world, stating:

> The only reliable interpretation of "human" lies in basic biology, an inherently limited category. The problem is that our mania for self-indulgent theorizing drives humans toward arrogance or even cavalier anthropocene supremacy about their biology. (Kingswell, 2023)

In this example, the *speculative posthuman* position advocates equal treatment of nonhuman and human entities.

The words of Nick Bostrom, philosopher and former head of the Future of Humanity Institute at Oxford University, are echoing the *critical posthuman* perspective, which seeks to deconstruct problematic framings of humans brought on through an anthropocentric focus. In an interview, he explained that a full shutdown of ChatGPT and AI innovation due to fear would be unethical. As Bostrom stated:

> If an AI showed signs of sentience, it plausibly would have some degree of moral status … This means there would be certain ways of treating it that would be wrong, just as it would be wrong to kick a dog or for medical researchers to perform surgery on a mouse without anesthetizing it. (Al-Sibai, 2023b)

Here, the *critical posthuman* position emphasizes the need to rethink how humans define and position humanity in our world.

Finally, the transhumanist perspective, which promotes the cultivation of the posthuman by any technological means, is evidenced in a statement by Ray Kurzweil. As co-founder of the Singularity Group, which advocates for accelerating technological innovation, he publicly spoke out against the "Future of Life" open letter. This letter, circulated in May 2023 by scientists, called for a pause in AI experimentation. Kurzweil felt their move to shut down research because of ethical concerns around a few technologies was far too drastic. He said:

> There are tremendous benefits to advancing AI in critical fields such as medicine and health, education, the pursuit of renewable energy sources to replace fossil fuels, and scores of other fields. I didn't sign because I believe we can address the signers' safety concerns in a more tailored way that doesn't compromise these vital lines of research. However, more nuance is needed to unlock AI's profound advantages to health and productivity while avoiding the real perils. (Koetsier, 2023)

Here, the *transhumanist view* emphasizes that while technology can be a downside, for some, the benefits of technological advancement outweigh those perceived risks. While there is no single agreed-upon definition or representation of posthumanism, in general, this philosophical approach has several shared areas of conceptual concern. These include challenging traditional definitions of humanity, stressing the evolutionary nature of the world, and the importance of embracing and advocating technological innovation and advancement. Also, two common lines of argumentation exist within posthumanist discussions about our human future. One focuses on the technical augmentation or transformation of the human condition, while the other is primarily concerned with the cultural critiques of traditional categories used to define humanity.

The Human-Technology Relationship and the Divine

Now, we focus on how these perspectives on posthumanism surface within media discourse about the human-technology relationship and how such discussions often use religious language to describe this connection. In the rest of Section 3, I argue that news media, explicitly and implicitly, frequently rely on one of three depictions of the human relationship to technology, which uses spiritual language and assumptions to explain this relationship. This argument is based on media framing theory, which asserts that the way information is presented by media directly influences how people will understand it (De Vreese, 2005). Framing theory is often used in communication and media studies to identify common strategies journalists and editors use to present facts or events so that they are read and interpreted in a certain way (Weaver, Lively & Bimbe 2009). Framing theory also argues that the media play a powerful role in shaping public opinion about current events. Here, the idea that media often use one of three frames about the human-technology relationship in their reporting about technological innovations directly connects to different posthumanist assumptions.

Over the past three decades, I have followed conversations about the posthuman from the realm of philosophy to becoming ideals evoked by technology designers and futurists when they talk about the manifest destiny of our technological future. During this time, I have also seen posthumanism become an ideology manifest and driving the backstory of many popular media films centered around technology (Campbell, 2016; Hauskeller, Philbeck & Carbonell, 2015), the news coverage of science-related policy decisions (Fox & Alldred, 2020), and as a framework for explaining emerging technology (Carlson, 2016).

In my research, I have also argued that this widespread use and implicit acceptance of our coming posthuman future have begun to shape even religious groups' thinking and discussions of information and digital technologies (Campbell, 2016b, 2021). This can especially be seen in how Christian leaders and clergy during the COVID-19 global pandemic constructed what I call a "technological apologetic." This is a public narrative used to justify their technology use and to explain their move to online worship services when face-to-face meetings were no longer possible due to health and safety concerns (Campbell & Jones, 2022). I suggest several of the pro-technology arguments commonly used by religious leaders to explain and justify their digital media use for ministry purposes, have posthuman roots.

Next, I present three common frames about human-technology relationships, which suggest an unspoken inevitable acceptance of the posthuman outlook. I suggest these narratives illustrate the posthuman-inspired conception of how the human condition is seen to intersect with technological innovation. I argue that these draw attention to underlying assumptions about the divine in a technological world. I further this by arguing that using religious symbolism and language is not exclusive to people of faith. Much of the discourse about the potentials of posthumanism carries a strong mystical or religious-like quality.

The Technology-Cultured Frame: Technology Is Informing Humanity and Its Future

A popular narrative within the posthuman discourse on technology and culture asserts that developments are pushing humanity toward a future where the human form will eventually give way to a new technologically mediated existence. In *The Posthuman Manifesto* (2005), Pepperell asserted technological advancements have created a world that is no longer human-centered, as "all technological progress of human society is geared toward the transformation of the human species" (2005, Postulate 1.2). He further suggests that "our being is embodied in an extended technological world" (2005, Postulate 8.8). The narrative focuses not only on the perceived human need to embrace technology but also posits technological experimentation as the basis for understanding our evolving human world. It suggests human-technological assimilations are a given as humans move toward a new technological state of being that will displace the centrality of human culture.

The human form is thus seen as a less desirable state. This echoes Roden's "critical posthumanism" position, which seeks to deconstruct the human subject and privileges emerging technological forms. Such narratives of an inevitable technologically driven future prioritize technology's role in cultural development over humans shaping society. It asserts technology has the power to transform human existence. This echoes discussions from Section 1 of technology as a powerful tool that can change the direction of the human world. It also presents technology as an instrument to engage more fully with technological innovation, which is perceived as beneficial to humanity.

This I call the "technology-cultured" frame, presenting technology as the superior partner in the human-technology relationship. Posthumanity is best explained by embracing emerging technologies whose values will lead our future. This optimistic view of technology evokes ideas of technology being akin to a spiritual or god-like force, able to transform humanity for the better. This perspective was used to report churches' engagement with technology during the COVID-19 pandemic (Campbell & Jones, 2022). Digital technology was described as a" bridge" connecting churches to a new worship "space" and "reality" through the embrace of online services (Campbell & Jones, p. 213). Technology provides religious congregations access to new multimedia tools and spaces, which allows them to be more flexible in their forms of gathering and ways of connecting with the members during the global pandemic

By prioritizing the role and influence of emerging technologies in society, the technology-cultured frame advocates humanity to use network technologies because of the powerful opportunities they offer humans. This frame highlights how networked technologies can restructure our social and even religious realities and everyday lives for the better.

Enhanced-Human Frame: Humanity Should Embrace Technological Affordances for Their Benefits

The next narrative, the enhanced-human frame, asserts that understanding the evolution of humanity augmented by technology must begin by evaluating our current human state and reconceiving it in new ways. This connects to what Roden (2015) calls "speculative posthumanism," which opposes human-centered thinking about technology but also recognizes any form of "technological singularity," or human-machine mixing, can only be seen as a descendant of current humans. This narrative suggests conceptions of the posthuman must acknowledge the fact that technology will enhance human attributes in unforeseen directions. This means the traditional markers of being a rational human may be lost in our technological evolution. In this way, the human-technology hybrid offers a chance to overcome human limitations. However, the choice to move down this path does not necessarily present an equal integration of human technology.

This discourse employs the "enhanced-human" frame, focusing on the affordance offered by new technologies to extend human abilities. While the enhanced human frame emphasizes embracing new technologies, its rationale is firmly situated on doing so for the betterment of humanity. This frame presents technology as being more than a tool. Here, technology becomes a set of techniques or systems of unique practices that create opportunities and risks. Technology is praised as being able to help humans move past their weaknesses and sicknesses, and can be seen as opening doors to new manifestations of humanity. This position also connects with the idea of technology as industrialization, the promise that technology will enact change and transform social patterns that make human lives better. Yet within that promise is a hint of doubt and even fear of what that change could mean for humanity.

This discourse employs the "enhanced-human" frame, focusing on the affordance offered by new technologies to extend human abilities. While the enhanced-human frame emphasizes embracing new technologies, its rationale is firmly situated in doing so for the betterment of humanity. The enhance-human frame often appeared in media coverage of pandemic churches discussing their transition to online services when they quoted leaders who enthusiastically integrated digital media and online worship for the first time (Campbell & Jones, 2022). Quotes often stressed how pastors felt they were better off for their embrace of the internet because it allowed them to become an enhanced church, one with more communicative potential and stronger communal bonds by moving from offline to online worship experiences that allowed them to strengthen their members who often felt afraid or isolated during the pandemic.

This frame often highlights that technological opportunities offer humans advantages beyond the limits of a traditional embodied culture. Humans are called to embrace technology because of its unique affordances, allowing them to become a better version of themselves. This frame acknowledges that the human state is already being enhanced by technology and asks, Why not simply embrace the potential opportunities offered by technology? This frame emphasizes humanity's need to adopt technology because of the innate limits of the human form (sickness, death, etc.); it stresses technology can help humans overcome such perceived weaknesses by embracing the empowering affordance of digital technology.

Human-Technology Hybrid Frame: Humanity Merges with Technology

The third narrative, the "human-technology hybrid" frame, emphasizes how certain human characteristics of humanity can be complimented and abilities extended through technology, creating not just a new relationship but potentially a new existence. The "human-technology hybrid" frame creates a new in-betweenness, where memories and hints of humanity may linger in a technologically transformed state of being.

Roden (2015) and others describe these arguments as the "transhumanist" narratives, which focus on how technological enhancements can aid and advance human capabilities. This narrative draws on definitions that present the posthuman as "someone or an entity whose basic capacities so radically exceed those of un-augmented humans as to be best thought of as constituting a new kind of being" (World Transhumanist Association FAQ, 2001). Transhuman discourse focuses on engaging and adopting various bio-, digital, and nanotechnologies that enable humanity to enter a new transitional state. The *Transhumanist Declaration* (1998), supported by numerous posthuman groups, emphasizes redesigning the human condition by embracing enhancement technologies through responsible rational planning. This is to influence the "well-being of all sentience."

Overall, transhumanists believe in the moral right to extend life, enhance mental and physical capabilities, and embrace new technologies aiding these progressions while exercising ongoing reflection about the future. This connects to Section 1, which sees technology as a novelty, though arguably promotes an overoptimistic view of the technological transformation of humanity. The transhumanist perspective states that posthumans will "emerge via modified biological descent" and yet be seen as "recursive extensions of AI technologies" (Roden, 2015, p. 22). This suggests a new relationship between humans and technology and the creation of a hybrid form, carrying characteristics of human predecessors while existing as radically new technological successors. Roden's speculative posthumanist narrative posits that future posthuman forms will be unique, blurring previous humanity with new technological forms.

Here, we see technology as a mode of knowing at play; technology can change humans' practices and abilities and even transform physical beings into something more than human. This new entity has remnants of the human but will differ greatly in its identity, composition, and outlook. The posthuman evolution often evokes both theistic and nontheistic notions of divinity. As technology opens the door to humanity becoming something more than itself, posthumanists draw on the image of humans emerging as god-like, acquiring all-knowing trans-present abilities through actions such as brain-downloading onto a computer or at least becoming a superhuman entity through implants. This kind of techno-utopian idealism also showed up in some religious leaders' discourse about the promises technologies offered churches during the COVID-19 pandemic. Pastors described technology as "opening the door" to become "a new kind of church" able to transcend traditional limitations of time and space to grow their congregations beyond the limits of their local geography

(Campbell & Jones, 2022). This allowed them to expand their congregations through cross-country and international visitors and gave them a "global vision" for what their church could be.

The human-technology hybrid frame emphasizes how various characteristics of humanity and technology interrelate and inform one another, creating not just a new relationship but potentially a new existence. This frame closely relates to current discussions within Digital Religion studies, highlighting the need to carefully consider the interplay of the digital (or online) and traditional (or offline) culture and the ways it creates a new, blurred social reality (Campbell, 2013). The space between the online and offline is often described as a "third space," where spaces intersect with liminal social spaces to create a new conceptual space that emerges at the intersection of two established terrains (Oldenburg, 1989).

How These Human-Technology Frames Point to Spiritual Understandings of Our Technological World

The discussion about posthumanism and different perspectives and positions taken in posthumanist philosophy leads up to this identification and a discussion of common frameworks used to depict how technological advancements reshape human existence and identity. Each of the frames presented – the technology-cultured frame, the enhanced-human frame, and the human-technology hybrid Frame – offers a distinct perspective on notable concerns within posthumanism, especially technology's influence on cultural and societal development, human enhancement, and the merging of human and technological forms.

The "technology-cultured frame" views technology as the dominant force in shaping humanity and its future, displacing the centrality of human culture and redefining human existence in a technologically mediated state. This frame employs concepts of transcendence, often portraying technology as an almost divine force that transforms humanity and enables it to surpass traditional human limitations akin to a spiritual evolution or destiny.

The "enhanced-human frame" focuses on using technology to enhance human physical and mental capacities, advocating for the moral right to use technology to improve human life and progress toward a better future. The language of enhancement used in this frame resonates with themes of salvation and redemption, suggesting that technology offers a path to overcome the limitations of the human condition, much like religious doctrines promising transformation or enlightenment.

The "human-technology hybrid frame" envisions a hybrid existence where humanity and technology are intertwined, leading to a new state of being that carries elements of both human and technological predecessors while creating a radically new form of existence. This idea of a hybrid existence mirrors mystical or liminal states in spirituality, where boundaries between the material and the transcendent blur, creating a "third space" that echoes sacred or transformative thresholds.

Each of these frames explores the human-technology relationship through unique lenses but shares a reliance on spiritual or religious imagery to articulate their visions of transformation. The technology-cultured frame elevates technology to a central, almost divine status, emphasizing humanity's submission to its transformative power. It parallels narratives of divine omnipotence where an external force beyond their control reshapes humans. The enhanced human frame, by contrast, positions technology as a tool for self-directed salvation, where humans actively use technological "gifts" to transcend their physical and mental limitations – reminiscent of spiritual practices aimed at achieving perfection or enlightenment. Finally, the human-technology hybrid frame delves into the liminal, depicting a fusion that creates a new "being," much like mystical states or spiritual rebirths that dissolve and reconfigure boundaries between the physical and spiritual.

All three frames use religious or spiritual language to describe humanity's journey with technology, suggesting a deeply transformative process akin to rites of passage, enlightenment, or transcendence. While each frame varies in its interpretation of technology's role, whether dominant, cooperative, or integrative, they converge in portraying it as a force capable of fundamentally reshaping the essence of what it means to be human.

The discussion earlier highlights how the human-technology relationship is frequently framed using religious and spiritual language, emphasizing concepts like transcendence, salvation, and transformation. This framing not only shapes how technology is perceived – as a force akin to the divine – but also invites deeper reflection on humanity's pursuit of meaning and progress through technological advancements. By linking technology to spiritual ideals, these narratives influence contemporary discussions about God and technology, raising questions about the role of faith, morality, and ultimate purpose in an increasingly technologized world.

Summarizing How Different Media Discourses Shape Technology Religiously

Sections 2 and 3 of this Element demonstrated different ways media discourses about emerging technologies, humans, and understandings of God/gods may use religious and spiritual metaphors and ideals in those multimedia discourses. When focusing on how popular films depict the once futuristic world of artificial intelligence, we see how science fiction films present or equate these technologies with spiritual and religious traits. Science fiction films offer a rich repository for considering how scholars' understanding of the relationship between religion and technology is visualized, performed, and conceptually embraced in popular media culture. Then, by investigating posthuman philosophy and how this outlook frames the human relationship to technology, contemporary debates and advocacy about AI surrounding ChatGPT suggest very different views about the future of the human world. The conceptual push to evolve beyond humanity and to become technologically enhanced nonhumans offers us a way to insert spiritual considerations into posthuman discourse.

Bringing together these separate conversations and different approaches to human and religious interactions with contemporary and emerging technology, a set of common narratives about the human-divine-technology intersection begins to surface. Identifying and unpacking these narratives is the focus of the final section of this Element.

4 Models for Understanding the Created Relationship between God and Technology

In the last two sections of this Element, I have discussed different religious myths and frames used to talk about the potential and promise of technology, I have sought to demonstrate the close connections between technology and religious beliefs or concepts in popular media discourse. It is important to note that the classifications presented in this Element are not exhaustive, nor are they the only categories scholars might use to describe how spiritual and religious ideas manifest themselves within discourses about technology. Rather, these case studies and the correlating taxonomies emerging from them are offered as common and illustrative examples of how language, religion, and spirituality are used to interpret technology's goals, motivations, and potential outcomes in contemporary society. Considering how religion and spirituality are applied in varied technological discourses helps us identify how the relationship between God and technology is commonly conceived. Looking at these different categories together helps to create a platform for a shared conversation about the impact of religious metaphors and spiritual myths on contemporary debates about the nature of digital technologies and AI.

In this final section of the Element, the previous case studies and classifications are brought into conversation with each other so that overlapping themes can be seen. This work identifies and names four conceptual models to capture the core assumption about the relationship between God and technology. I believe these models can be useful in academic and popular media discourses about how religion and spirituality manifest in our technological culture. These models are often implicitly used by journalists, media critics, and digital influencers to praise and condemn technology from religious and secular positions. To set the stage for introducing these four models, we must first look backward at how the conversation in this Element has evolved and where it has conceptually brought us. This requires a brief revisit of the religious myths and frames highlighted in the Element thus far.

A Review of Concepts and Commonalities in Religious Discussion about Technology

In the introduction of *God and Technology*, I discussed the common ways the concepts of technology and God have been conceived within religious discourse about technology. It began with looking at technology, which, on a very basic level, can refer to a tool used to create or perform a certain task, a technique or skill that is linked to its design and intentions, or a form of knowledge that informs a distinct culture that influences its use. I highlighted McOmber's three narratives about technology being about – instrumentality (a neutral tool influenced by its use), industrialization (a pessimistic view of technology as a disrupter), or novelty (an optimistic view of technology as a cultural transformer). Each view represents a specific set of beliefs about values or intentions seen to stand behind technology. These views of technology were highlighted throughout the Element to show how they are embedded within different categorizations of technology discussed. These views could also be seen as influencing different arguments about technology's perceived nature in these discussions.

The introduction highlighted different understandings of God underlying various religious discussions about technology. These range from seeing God as a supreme being, an idea deeply rooted in Western Judeo-Christian views, to utilizing the idea of god as a revered deity and/or a divine/spiritual force, which may draw on Eastern religious traditions' understandings. I argued much of the historical discourse about religion and technology, especially coming out of the philosophy of technology, has drawn on Christian theology and symbolism. However, I also noted a rise in the use of Eastern religious imagery and concepts, especially from Buddhism, employed in late twentieth- and early twenty-first-century scholarly discourse about computer and network technology and in popular media representations. This means being aware of the roots of the conception of God, being engaged in discussions about technology becomes increasingly important, requiring a deeper awareness of the underlying assumptions guiding how technology is seen to act as a spiritual source or even being.

Central to discussions in *God and Technology* is the presentation of two case studies exploring the different ways religious ideas and language have informed the discussion of the spiritual aspects of technology. In Section 2, the conceptual deification of technology is explored by considering the prominent religious stories about technology promoted through AI-focused films. Here, three techno-spiritual myths were presented: technological transcendence (AI empowering humans with divine qualities), technological mysticism (technology engagement is a form of religious practice), and techgnosis (technology evolves to become a god or god-like). These demonstrate that the power and potential of emerging technologies are often equated with spiritual qualities that shape the human experience as we engage with them.

In Section 2 the discussion turned to posthuman philosophy, and the positions taken within posthumanism regarding their interpretation of cause-effect relationships between technology and human evolution. This case study focused on different predictions of the human-technology relationship in a posthuman future and the religious nuances within these discourses. The "technology-culture" frame presents humans being shaped by the prevalence of technology in culture, as technology holds the power position in the relationship. The "enhanced-human" frame focuses on the benefits of technology in extending human abilities. The "human-technology hybrid" frame emphasizes the human embrace of technology to take on a new existence. These frames highlight the inevitable technological transformation of human form, outlook, and identity. At the heart of these case studies is the assertion that human engagement with technology shapes our experience and understanding of the material world in ways that can be easily described and understood through the language of religion and spiritual encounters (Campbell, 2016).

While each case study focused on a different intersection between technology, religion, and humanity, they share some common assumptions. The character of technology can be seen as sharing some of the same traits associated with the Western Christian conception of God. Technology is portrayed as a powerful, intelligent, unique entity that has played a transformative role in human history and is seen as actively directing the future. This equating technology with the image of a singular, commanding, and authoritative God over the human world also opens the door for its critique. Secular criticism of God as an invisible being that is fallible, detached, uncaring, and/or even an adversary of humanity can be easily applied to the idea of technology, especially when it is equated as being an all-powerful monolithic culture-shaping entity or force. These links suggest handholds within our historical thinking and cultural assumptions about the nature of technology and the values behind it that need to be further considered. To continue to move toward identifying the commonalities between these religious myths, and the frames presented, we now need to revisit some previous discussions from the philosophy of technology.

Religious Metaphors about Technology from the Philosophy of Technology

As noted in the introduction, scholars in the philosophy of technology have long approached technology as a value-laden enterprise, and religious discourse has played an important role in building this claim. Going back to the nineteenth century, Karl Marx, a notable skeptic of religion, argued the need for critical reflection on technology and religion's impact on humanity, its actions, and thinking. Marx evoked a religious tone when he asserted that it was "much easier to discover by analysis the earthly kernel of the misty creations of religion than to do the opposite" (1867), suggesting that the world proposed by science and religion was not without scrutiny. While Marx rejected the importance or centrality of religion in the central public life, he did not deny that religion offered poignant ideas or imagery with which one could describe facets of the natural world.

The use of religious metaphors to describe both the opportunities and challenges technology poses to the human social and political spheres has been a recognizable theme within certain strains of the philosophy of technology literature. In the twentieth century, Martin Heidegger argued that attempts at human control over technology could be equated with a spiritual act, and technology could be understood as having a "saving power" (Heidegger, 1977, p. 28) that even God may be at risk of becoming subordinate to. Jacques Ellul also wrote about what he saw as the functional religious character and quality of technology (or what he referred to as technique) and its increasing ability to become the object of humanity's spiritual devotion. "Since the religious object is that which is uncritically worshipped, technology tends more and more to become the new god" (Wilkinson 1964, p. xi). More recently, Carl Mitcham (1986) argued that Christian theology had made notable contributions to the rise of modern technology by providing language that points to the moral purposes it can serve for the betterment of humanity. As Mitcham argues, "God communicates to humans a higher vision, and thus collaborates with them in transcending their technological limitations" (Mitcham, 2022, p. 6). From such examples, it is noted that the philosophy of technology has often approached technology as a value-laden enterprise. Evoking spiritual language allowed scholars to describe technological engagement as a struggle over competing values of power, control, and efficiency promoted by technology.

Further, using religious language, metaphors, and ideals to describe technologies as both a threat and a tool of promise is not just evident in the philosophy of technology literature. Scholars in the philosophy of communication and media studies have also drawn on this perceived connection between spirituality and technology. In his work on the commodification of art (1936) and research into the capitalist production cycle (1989), Walter Benjamin referred to how he perceived the relationship between religion and technology. He argued that religiosity and technology were human-centered enterprises and must be considered and understood. He uses the religious notion of the word "demonic" about technology that has been hybridized so that such artifacts and their reciprocal relationships no longer fit into clear categories of material versus living structures (Cohen, 1989). Demonic technologies create new dimensions and spaces where religion and technology meet and transgress traditional boundaries that complicate our secular dualisms (NA, 2012).

In the twenty-first century, this tendency to evoke spiritual concepts or beliefs to describe the influence and control of information and communication technologies has continued. John Durham Peters speaks about this perceived overlap between the natural and spiritual worlds in his book *Speaking into the Air* (1999). In his writing about the idea of "word-magic" found in early human culture, naming an object gives the individual inherent power over it. Peter's understanding of language as a form of technology endowed with "contagious magic" (Peters, 1999, p. 239). Drawing on Elaine Eisenstein's study (1980) of the rise of the printing press and its interaction with religious discourse, he suggests describing communication technologies as infused with otherworldly powers is not foreign within this tradition of scholarship. In recent years, scholars have drawn parallels, between digital media technologies' ability to evoke spiritual ideals and practices within their users. For example, Eng Hui Lim (2018) suggests that the emerging information communication technologies have led to the manifestation of "digital spirits" or new religious beings and forms of deity to emerge among us. In his book *Technologies of Religion* (2016), Sam Han argues that digital media forces us to rethink the secularization thesis of modernity, which posits that in a world dominated by science and technology, innovations, ideology, religious authority, and influence continue to diminish. Instead, he states the post-secular turn has ushered in a reclaiming of spiritual logic that allows the sacred and secular to coexist and complement one another.

With digital media's continued influence and importance within Western culture in the twenty-first century and the rise of new technologies such as augmented reality and artificial intelligence, the tendency to equate technological engagement with religious pursuits has only strengthened. It has become common to use myths that link human-created technologies to some higher, transcendent purpose or outcome. This brief review notes several tendencies related to the use of religious language and spiritual references, especially from the Judeo-Christian tradition, about the technological enterprise. First, references are often made to how technologies mimic the traits or actions of religious entities – such as God, spirits, and demons – and to describe the influence of technology upon humanity. Second, religious concepts such as belief in "salvation" or "transcendence" are often used to communicate technology's powerful nature and abilities. Third, and finally, interference is made that the effect of technology on people and society can be interpreted as having a mystical or magic-like quality. Highlighting these tendencies is important because they echo the techno-spiritual myths discussed. Within these myths lie important language and images, which will lead us to a discussion of models of how God, as both a divine entity and spirit, is seen to intersect with different beliefs about technology.

The Religious Rhetoric of the Techno-Spiritual Myths

In Section 2, three myths about technology's spiritual nature or qualities were presented, which I argue inform the storylines of many contemporary popular sci-fi films. These films typically depict a range of outcomes of human engagement with new technologies, each evoking distinct assumptions about the future of humanity and the spiritual nature of technologies. In short, these spiritual myths show that technology will endow humanity with superhuman or supernatural abilities, become a god-like spiritual force influencing humanity, or offer humans a religious context or state to which they can ascend. Each techno-spiritual myth was linked to one of three narratives about technology and religion from books authored in the late 1990s.

David Noble argued that religious belief had emerged around technology, and considered this technological worship to have societal implications and ethical consequences. He described the end goal of the religion of technology as "technological transcendence," a speculative future where technology offers humanity transformative potential to extend its capabilities and existence. Erik Davis offered the concept of "techgnosis" to describe the influence of religious and mystical traditions on the development of digital culture. He uses the term "gnosis" to refer to spiritual knowledge or insight that can be gained through direct experience with technology. In other words, Davis suggests technology can be a conduit for spiritual experiences and the exploration of profound questions about the nature of existence. Finally, William Stahl presented the concept of "technological mysticism," where traditional religious beliefs are replaced by trust and faith in the capabilities of technology and human innovation. Here, technology assumes a quasi-religious status in society because it provides a new source of meaning and a platform for spiritual exploration. Each of the authors offers a distinct narrative about the potential impact of technology on our religious and spiritual lives, which informs the models about the relationship between god and technology presented here.

However, I argue there is a fourth archetype for the relationship between god and technology that needs to be considered, which is inferred but not explicitly addressed by these authors. Here, Kevin Kelly's book *What Technology Wants* (2010) offers important insights into an understanding of technology that extends not just the human body and its abilities but the evolution of the mind and spirit. Kelly, the co-founder of *Wired* magazine, introduces us to the idea of the "technium," which he claims is a new reality that technology itself is pushing us toward, one where the ethos of technology seeks to achieve its desired end goal. That goal is to foster progress and human betterment and even offer us a "portrait of God." He describes emerging technologies as unique beings, our "technological children," which need to be trained and programmed with positive human values because of technologie's innate desire to evolve and advance beyond our current imagination.

Four Models for Discussing the Relationship between God and Technology

All the arguments and evidence presented in *God and Technology* bring us to this final discussion.

I assert that four models can sum-up the relationship between God/gods and technology in contemporary media discourse. Each model combines a distinct understanding of the nature and purpose of technology, intersecting with different interpretations of who or what "god" is and is seen to represent in our technology-driven culture. The models discussed include:

(1) technology makes humans god-like,
(2) technology bestows the power of the gods (magic, a divine force),
(3) technology offers humans an encounter with god (spiritual experience), and
(4) technology itself is a god.

Next, each of these models is described and contextualized about the core arguments put forward by the authors highlighted earlier.

Their presence in current media discourse is also illustrated by looking at how these models are used to support and critique technology in 2023 news coverage of developments in artificial intelligence. In July 2023, journalist Steve Rose conducted five interviews with different international experts on AI for an article published in the British newspaper *The Guardian*. The interview feature aimed to highlight arguments about the specific ways artificial intelligence technology could improve the world by addressing issues of poverty, climate change, and medical advancements. Interestingly, four of the individuals quoted in this article present rhetorical arguments supporting the further development of AI that echo each of the models in this section. These examples are followed by editorial and opinion pieces that are critical of AI, which also draws on claims about the relationship between God and technology put forth by these conceptual models.

Technology Makes Humans God-like

The first conceptual model presents technology engagement as allowing humanity to become divine or god-like. Innovative features of technology are described as enabling and empowering humanity in new ways. The underlying argument is that technology allows humans to become something more than they are. The language used often infers that technology provides a gateway to salvation from the world's brokenness and human limitations. This idea was evoked in previous discussions about transhumanism and its goal of evolving to become something more than human, the posthuman. It is also articulated in the sci-fi myth of technological transcendence, where technology offers human god-like abilities.

Simply put, this model suggests that humanity becomes god-like by embracing technology. It presents technology as having an eschatological component that can restore humanity to its original state of perfection. This is echoed in Noble's thesis about the "religion of technology" (1999), where human engagement with technology is seen as an attempt to regain some lost sense of divinity, meaning, and control over the world. It assumes technology possesses redemptive qualities, allowing humanity to return to some pure state in which it was divinely empowered. Yet, as Noble suggests, this idea is based on a false premise where humanity is deceived into thinking technology will provide lost powers that it never actually possessed. This model raises questions about the nature of humanity or what it means to be human in a technological world.

This "technology makes humans god-like" model is often used to promote technology development and engagement because of the superhuman abilities it offers us. Rejecting or refusing to use technology is framed as an illogical choice. It asserts that technology is good for humanity because humans are made to become something more than they currently are. Embracing technology makes us better versions of ourselves and the evolved beings we are meant to become. In the article "Five Ways AI Could Improve the World: 'We Can Cure All Diseases, Stabilize Our Climate, Halt Poverty'" (Rose, 2023), Ray Kurzweil, a well-known computer scientist and futurist, previously mentioned in this Element, evoked this idea when he argued humans should embrace, rather than fear, AI, because it offers us superhuman abilities. As Kurzweil states:

> Most movies about AI have an "us versus them" mentality, but that's not the case. This is not an alien invasion of intelligent machines; it's the result of our efforts to make our infrastructure and way of life more intelligent. It's part of human endeavor. We merge with our machines. Ultimately, they will extend who we are. (Rose, 2023)

Technology columnist John Davidson expresses the underlying claim that artificial intelligence empowers people with god-like abilities in the article "The Race to God-like AI and What It Means for Humanity," published in the *Financial Review*. Davidson, in contrast, argues this striving to embrace the superhuman potential of AI could come with consequences:

> There's the moving from where we are now to AGI (artificial general intelligence). And then there's the move from AGI, which is sort of human-level intelligence, to God-level intelligence. And once it hits God AI level or, also known as superhuman machine intelligence – SMI for another acronym – once it gets there, we really don't know what might happen. And that's when a lot of researchers think that human extinction might be on the cards. (Murray, 2023)

Technology is praised and critiqued because it pushes humanity beyond "recursive self-improvement." It represents a giving-over or take-over of humans through technology. Davidson's concerns echo Noble's criticisms of the "religion of technology" as he notes the otherworldly evolution often promoted by technology designers encourages a false enchantment in the guise of a technological fix. While technology may extend current human abilities, the need or desire to become god-like to redeem a broken world seems an overly optimistic view of the technological-human.

Technology Bestows the Power of the Gods

The second model presents technology as a kind of spiritual or divine force offered to humanity. Here, technology is presented as a mighty medium possessing magical powers. It differs from the belief that technology can make humans god-like in that the magic of technology is not transferred to humans. Instead, power stays with the technology itself. Humans are offered the opportunity to use the dominance of technology only when wielding or engaging with the artifact. Technology is framed as possessing or being host to a supernatural force that humanity can use. This model suggests God or god's power resides within technology but can be accessed by those who embrace and use it. It echoes some of the ideas of critical posthumanism discussed in the previous section, which privileges the advancement of technologies and emerging technological forms over humans.

This model is like Davis's description or myth of "techgnosis", which suggests its mystical impulses and god-like powers of technology that have sparked the Western world's obsession. Like the model illustrating that technology makes humans god-like, it asserts that humans have somehow lost their god-like command throughout history. The pursuit of technological use and development allows them to reclaim them. The perceived sway of technology also encourages its users to anthropomorphize it or to frame it as a supernatural force or spirit guide empowering humanity when aligned with it. This drive to partner with technology to use its power can easily morph into the fourth model discussed, where technology is seen as a god to worship.

David Rolnick, a professor and Chair in AI at McGill University, uses rhetoric that evokes this model in his discussion of the speculative future of technology to address issues of Climate Change. He stresses that humanity is currently helpless in fixing the current degradation of our physical world. However, with the help of new AI, humans might have a fighting chance to survive. As Rolnick asserts:

> Climate change is already killing people, and many more people are going to die, even in a best-case scenario, but we get to decide now just how bad it gets. Action taken decades from now is much less valuable than action taken soon. Thinking of AI as a futuristic tool that will lead to immeasurable good or harm is a distraction from the ways we can and are using AI tools right now and what we can do to align them with what's best for society. (Rose, 2023)

The supernatural powers of AI technology, used wisely by humanity, are framed as offering at least partial salvation from climate destruction. Multiple examples can be found of AI advocates likening AI technology to magic. The famous quote by Arthur C. Clarke states, "Any sufficiently advanced technology is indistinguishable from magic." This is frequently referred to by AI advocates seeking to promote its use in various industries and professions. "AI feels like magic," states one journalist describing how generative AI technologies are being used by public relations professionals to create current promotional campaigns (Carter, 2023). One computer engineer also frames AI as helping professionals recapture lost magical qualities of hardware design, stating: "AI, we finally have the tool we need to take the 'hard' out of 'hardware' and put the magic back into the design process" (Cassidy, 2023).

In these examples, individuals emphasize that technology possesses magical potential to transform their jobs. By embracing AI innovations, they have new supernatural abilities that can transform their work. This model of technology, seeing technology as offering humans god-like authority, becomes an important rhetoric used by AI advocates. It is used not just to express individuals' excitement about technology, but it is perceived to contain the ability to heal broken parts of our world.

Technology Offers a Spiritual Experience

A third model or way to show how the relationship between god and technology can be represented is to frame human engagement with technology as a gateway to a magical or spiritual experience. Here, descriptions of technology stress that technology possesses a mystical or even transcendental quality. Technology use is seen as transporting humanity to a new space or state where they can experience the supernatural. This emphasizes a belief that technology offers humans a place of encounter with the metaphysical realm or even the divine. This is because technology can alter our minds, expanding our knowledge and human consciousness. This model suggests that technology and its use open the door to a new, more enlightened reality. Embracing new technologies can allow humans to engage in the spirit realm beyond human limitations or expand their consciousness. This reflects ideas like the myth of "technological mysticism," which suggests that humans' reliance on technology mirrors religious-like behavior. Human engagement with technology is presented as putting one's trust in technological systems that can transport humans to otherworldly spaces or experiences that help them evolve beyond their current reality.

This "technological mysticism" is what Stahl described as humans putting "faith in the universal efficacy of technology" (Stahl, 1999, p. 13). In this way, technological use becomes part of a belief system that gives meaning and purpose to one's life by drawing humans from the mundane every day into a new reality full of hope. This sets up technology to become a form of devotion or even an expression of implicit religion, where practices and beliefs surrounding technology strongly resemble religion's role in society. In other words, technology engagement takes on a religious-like quality, giving users symbols and rituals that they endow with meaning and offer the promise of transcendence.

Approaching technology with the implicit assumption that it offers humans the ability to transform their reality and future is evident in many AI advocates' framing of this technology. For example, Ajeya Cotra, senior AI research analyst at Open Philanthropy, suggested that new intelligent AI systems can offer people a unique experience with a wise and "infinitely patient teacher," which could transform our educational system and learning processes.

> When you zoom out and look at where humanity has come from, on the scale
> of centuries and millennia, freedom, health, and equality have been getting
> better over time, and better technology has played a huge part in that. Truly
> advanced AI systems could continue that story – they could be more than just
> another technology; they could automate and radically accelerate the process
> of technological progress itself. In just a couple of decades, humanity could
> get to the kind of advanced future that feels like it's hundreds or thousands of
> years away. (Rose, 2023)

Here, technology is framed as a door that has always offered us access to greater knowledge and expanded our minds. It argues that the system extends this trajectory and speeds up our human advancement and growth. However, much of the criticism of AI is also based on concern for the reality that it opens to humanity. In an editorial in the *Financial Times,* Eithne Kennedy, Founder and CEO of Isle of Us in Singapore, states her concern about developers' claims that AI will expand our human creativity and spirituality. Kennedy argued in her editorial:

> I came away from the interview feeling nourished and grateful that humanity
> can most certainly surpass AI when it comes to innovative thought and
> spiritual enrichment as long as we stay alert and aware. As Acemoglu said:
> "Technological progress is the most important driver of human flourishing,
> but what we tend to forget is that the process is not automatic." This struck
> a chord with me: Will AI experience imposter syndrome when it is credited as
> being an "enhancer" of creativity? I hope so. (Kennedy, 2023)

The flaw is that the model assumes technological enhancement always brings human betterment and opens doors where our abilities and creativity are expanded rather than being controlled. While seeing technology as a door to spiritual expansion is one possibility, it is not the only option. This is why equating technology with positive spiritual advancement can be problematic.

Technology Is a God

The fourth and final model of the god-technology relationship emerging from the ideas and arguments explored in this Element is seeing technology as a god. Some hints point to this model in two of the techno-spiritual myths explored in Section 2 of the Element, especially the myths of technological transcendence, which suggest technology directs humans toward a god-like state, and technological mysticism, which promotes religious-like devotion to technology. The difference is that the model views technology itself as a god rather than suggesting humanity can leverage technology to become a god. This is also the most contentious framing of the god-technology relationship because it suggests technology becomes a substitute for god, a technological idol to be worshiped. This perspective offers the most compelling argument for embracing technology as a supreme, unquestionable entity.

This model links well to arguments put forth by Kevin Kelly in his book *What Technology Wants* (2010). In the book's final section, he argues that the evolutionary pulse that drives technology toward scientific advancement can be described as a "divine phenomenon that is a reflection of god." So, in the end, Kelly asserts that technology itself is not just a path to god but an extension of God itself. Kelly's narrative about our human future with technology is compelling, optimistic, and even theological. It suggests technological progress and growth are inevitable, as it has been programmed into the DNA or "conceptual essence" of current and emerging technologies. He offers the concept of the technium to describe the interconnected system of technology that surrounds our world and lives. While it started as an outgrowth of the human mind and creativity, it has now taken on a life of its own with the innate desire to perpetuate itself. Kelly's technium, therefore, is more than just god-like. It now exists as a deity itself. Technology functions as a supernatural force that continues to expand and grow more complex, and humanity must now learn to live in harmony with it.

This underlying assumption about the all-powerful nature of technology drives much of the argument for and against the further development of AI. Critics fear AI is now or beyond humans. While AI proponents are more measured in their assessments of these technology-independent abilities, they often recognize the inevitability of intelligent systems, suggesting learning how to collaborate with them to guide or shape AI's power.

Max Tegmark, a professor of physics and an AI researcher at MIT University, hints at this assumption and the emerging authority of AI technology. In Rose's article in *The Guardian*, he says that AI is more than just the next iteration of smart technologies. It possesses a unique supernatural potential that exceeds what humans could hope to accomplish in their lifetime. For Tegmark, AI offers humanity a new, transformative, and even idyllic future. As he said:

> We can cure all diseases, stabilize our climate, eliminate poverty, etc. We can flourish not just for the next election cycle but for billions of years. We have been on this planet for more than 100,000 years, and most of the time we have been like a leaf blowing around in the wind, without much control of our destiny, just trying to not starve or get eaten. Science, technology, and human intelligence have made us the captains of our own ship. I find that inspiring. If we can build and control superintelligence, we can quickly go from being limited by our own stupidity to being limited by the laws of physics. It could be the greatest empowerment moment in human history. (Rose, 2023)

The same hope that makes some advocates excited about the potential of AI to supersede current human intelligence has also raised panic, among others. In the article "Machine Learning Investor Warns AI Is Becoming Like a God," a journalist for *Futurism* magazine writes about the growing concern among some AI professionals and even investors. This is not just about what some call the abilities of a "god-like AI," but the fear that some have conceptually made AI into a god to be worshiped (Al-Sibai, 2023a). This rhetorical move consequently limits others' ability to offer critique or suggest regulations on the technology, for who can or should control god? The article quotes an opinion piece from the *Financial Times* by an AI investor, Ian Hogarth, about his fears that some already see AI as a god of a new religion. Hogarth states:

> A superintelligent computer that learns and develops autonomously, understands its environment without supervision, and can transform the world around it … "To be clear, we are not here yet," Hogarth continued. "But the nature of the technology means it is exceptionally difficult to predict exactly when we will get there. God-like AI could be a force beyond our control or understanding, and one that could usher in the obsolescence or destruction of the human race. (Al-Sibai, 2023a)

This model presents technology itself as a new god or a substitute for our previous conceptions of the divine. Such ideas raise concerns that human devotion to technology and progress is moving us toward worshiping a god of our own making. Rather than technology birthing a new religion, it can be seen as becoming a contemporary idol in a posthuman landscape.

Final Thoughts on God and Technology

From the offset of this Element, *God and Technology* aims to draw a historical and conceptual map about how and why religious language and ideals have become so intertwined with discourse about technology. The purpose of presenting these four distinct, yet overlapping, models about the relationship between ideas about the divine and technology is to create a platform for conversation on the current and potential implications of using religion to depict technology and represent its impact on humanity.

I believe these models, where technology can be seen – making humans god-like, possessing the power of the gods, offering a spiritual experience, and/or as a God – are often implicitly present within many academic discourses and public discussions about emerging media, as well as employed in media coverage about new technologies. I have suggested that ideas about God are often interlaced with various concepts of technology to advocate for or against human engagement with it. Model one presents technology as having the power of the divine in its qualities, which humans can harness to become god-like. Model two offers humans the control of the gods by partnering with and using technology. Model three suggests an engagement with technology offers humans a magical or spiritual experience that can be empowering and transformative. Finally, model four suggests that technology has become a deity that must be worshiped. These different intersections between technology and the metaphysical can provoke angst and awe from technology designers and user communities. These models have been used as rhetorical tools that present various views of our human future with technology. They have also been especially present in recent debates around artificial intelligence systems' future expansion and/or limitation.

These models emerge from a historical and contemporary analysis of discourses that arise when one looks at specific ways themes of religion, technology, and conceptions of God intersect. A narrative analysis of popular AI films not only revealed the perceived influence of technology on human culture but also pointed to a range of techno-spiritual myths used to equate emerging technologies with spiritual abilities. Then, by exploring different interpretations of the future offered by posthumanist philosophy, as illustrated in debates around AI chatbot technology, different versions of human-technology relationships are offered that also speak to how technology use has been infused with religious language and concepts. These different approaches and case studies offered in the Element not only provide insights into the different ways technology and ideas of religion and/or the divine can be seen to intersect, historically and in contemporary culture.

I suggest that by considering the common portrayals of God in digital media and communication presented here, alongside prominent spiritual myths about technology promoted by popular media, and in connection to how the human-technology relationship is framed through popular interpretations of posthuman views, several interesting conceptual overlaps begin to emerge. Together, these offer us a range of narratives with notable overlaps, which help us better understand how (and why) technological engagement has been represented as a spiritual or divine pursuit. Overall, I assert that these four models, presented in this final section, provide a spectrum of the most prominent conceptual framings of the relationship between god and technology in popular media culture and current public discourse. This is not to suggest that other models or narratives about God/gods and technology do not exist. However, identifying and creating a set of typologies for discussion inherently creates distinct boundaries and limits on such a discussion. However, I seek to offer an illustrative range of the discourses and conceptual frameworks that are easily identifiable in contemporary discussions about religion and technology for scholars to work with. These are offered as a suggested starting point for conversation and critique of the relationship between God, religion, and technology. This Element aims to help others interested in studying this intersection with an introductory map into this area of inquiry and categories that can be easily applied or interrogated about their work on studying religious and spiritual representation of technology in digital and emerging media cultures and contexts.

Besides offering categories and typologies – related to the philosophical study of technology and media discourses about religion – this Element draws attention to important shifts in popular understandings of religion's form, function, and role in contemporary culture. This Element echoes recent work in the study of media, religion, and culture studies, and digital religion studies, suggesting that the ways religion is seen and functions in technological and media contexts often differ from traditional understandings of religion. For example, in the current philosophy of technology discourses, religion is often assumed to be tied to a specific religious tradition, community, or institution. There is also a tendency in such reflection to conflate ideas about religion and spirituality or fail to differentiate them from such discourse. However, this Element shows that the form of religion is often highlighted in popular media discourses about how religion and technology are more often linked to expressions of lived religion, personalized interpretations and applications of traditional beliefs and practices, as well as forms of implicit religion, where traditionally secular activities or commitments are reinterpreted within a spiritual-religious framework (see Campbell & Tsuria, 2021). This fits sociologist Anthony Giddens's argument about religion, where he suggests that rather than declining in late-modern and postmodern society, we see an increased visibility of religion, but in a form different from traditional definitions and expression (Giddens, 1991). Scholars argue that what Giddens saw as an increased ability of individuals to self-define and express themselves in postmodern society is a tendency that also influences contemporary practices of religion (Besecke, 2001). As media and religion scholar Mia Lovheim has argued, religious identity has become part of "the project of the self," so individuals feel a greater sense of freedom to re-present and perform their identities in society in ways that are less constrained by traditional religious interpretations and ritual practices (Lovheim, 2013).

This trend toward "lived religion" was noted by scholars in the late twentieth and early twenty-first centuries, alongside increased public use of the internet, smartphones, and other emerging technologies in people's everyday lives and religious practices. The flexibility and personalization enabled by these networked media devices meant that technology could be used to create spaces where religious and spiritual meaning could be remixed. In the twenty-first century, technological engagement has increasingly become part of individuals expressing lived and implicit forms of religion. This Element raises attention to this and the need for greater awareness about how religion is defined and lived out in our technologically driven culture. For example, individuals increasingly argue in popular media that emerging technologies or their engagement can be seen as a form of religion. Without recognizing and understanding the shift in how religion is conceived and practiced in the twenty-first century, we cannot fully or accurately unpack such assertions. Popular claims that new technologies – such as artificial intelligence – will give birth to new religions are not at all new.

These different categories of God and technology discussed in this Element demonstrate the important role popular media and digital culture play, as re-interpreters of established theological concepts. The myths about technology highlighted in popular culture also frequently ascribe a divine origin or connection to technological advancements. These narratives depict technology as either an extension of the divine or as something that interacts with spiritual forces, shaping public perceptions of innovation and progress. Finally, we see that conceptualizing and depicting the relationship between humanity and technology in the media often are shown to have an inherently spiritual quality, suggesting that technological advancement is guiding humanity toward a new existential state with religious or transcendent significance. Across these different examples and perspectives, we see both religion and technology are framed as forces that shape human existence in profound ways. Each approach assumes that technology, like religion, has the power to influence, transform, or elevate humanity, often blurring the boundaries between the material and the spiritual.

When we consider these tendencies in a world driven by AI innovation, this suggests that as technology is increasingly integrated into society, media narratives about AI might also continue to rely on religious imagery to explain its position in or impact upon society., This means using the narrative that AI is either a divine force of progress or a potential source of existential transformation. This could shape public perception by amplifying hopes and fears about AI, casting it as either a tool for human transcendence or a force beyond human control. Such framing has the potential to influence policy debates, ethical considerations, and societal responses to AI, reinforcing ideas that AI is not just a technological tool but a phenomenon with profound, even spiritual, implications for humanity's future.

By shedding light on broader historical discourses and documented connections between ideas of religion and divine and technological innovation, I hope this Element will open a rich and fruitful discussion about how religious ideas are informing contemporary beliefs and predictions about our human future with technology. As scholars, our job is to uncover, name, and contextually explain the social and cultural conditions of our society and open a broader public discussion on these themes. I hope that those who read God and Technology will engage, interrogate, and take up the claims I have made about the conceptual and historical relationship between religion and technology and use them in their work to more fully explain how and why religion has and continues to inform our imagination and understanding of our increasingly technologized world.

References

Aguilar, Gabrielle, Campbell, Heidi, Stanley, Mariah, & Taylor, Ellen (2017). Communication mixed messages about religion through internet memes. *Information, Communication & Society*, 20(10), 1458–1520.

Albanese, Catherine L. (1999). *America: Religions and Religion* (3rd ed.). Belmont, CA: Wadsworth.

Al-Sibai, Noor (2023a). *Machine Learning Investor Warns AI is Becoming Like a God*. Futurism. https://futurism.com/ai-investor-agi-warning.

Al-Sibai, Noor (2023b). *Nick Bostrom Says AI Chatbots May Have Some Degree of Sentience*. The Byte. https://futurism.com/the-byte/nick-bostrom-ai-chatbot-sentience.

Ammerman, Nancy T. (2006). *Everyday Religion: Observing Modern Religious Lives*. Oxford: Oxford University Press. https://doi.org/10.1093/acprof:oso/9780195305418.001.0001.

Aristotle (2009). *Nicomachean Ethics*, Translated by D. Ross. Oxford University Press. (Original work 4th century BCE).

Armstrong, Karen (1993). *A History of God: The 4,000-Year Quest of Judaism, Christianity, and Islam*. New York City: Ballantine Books.

Aydin, Ciano & Verbeek, Peter-Paul (2015). *Transcendence in Technology*. *Techné: Research in Philosophy and Technology*, 19(3), 291–313. https://doi.org/10.5840/techne2015121742.

Bacon, Francis (1620). *Novum Organum*. John Bill.

Bailey, Edward (1997). *Implicit Religion in Contemporary Society*. Kampen, Netherlands: Kok Pharos Publishing House.

Bao, Jiemen (2005). Merit-making capitalism: Re-territorializing Thai Buddhism in Silicon Valley, California. *Journal of Asian American Studies*, 8(2), 115–142.

Beerman, Judy (2023). *Damon Lindelof's Mrs. Davis Is a Wild Allegory of Faith in the Age of AI*, Time Online. https://time.com/6271958/mrs-davis-review/.

Bellah, Robert N. (1970). *Beyond Belief: Essays on Religion in a Post-Traditional World*. New York: Harper & Row.

Bellar, Wendi, Campbell, Heidi, Cho, Kyong James, Terry, Andrea, Tsuria, Ruth, Yadlin-Segal, Aya, & Ziemer, Jordan (2013). Reading religion in internet memes. *Journal of Religion, Media & Digital Culture*. http://jrmdc.com/papers/2-2-bellar/.

Beniger, James (2009). *The Control Revolution: Technological and Economic Origins of the Information Society*. Cambridge, MA: Harvard University Press.

Benjamin, Walter (1936). *The Work of Art in the Age of Mechanical Reproduction.* New York City: Schocken Books.

Besecke, Kelly (2001). Speaking of meaning in modernity: Reflexive spirituality as a cultural resource. *Sociology of Religion, 62*(3), 365–381. https://doi .org/10.2307/3712355.

Bolter, Jay (2016). Posthumanism. In Robert T. Craig, Eric W. Rothenbuhler, Klaus Bruhn Jensen, & Jefferson D. Pooley, eds., *The International Encyclopedia of Communication Theory and Philosophy,* Indianapolis, IN: John Wiley & Sons, 1–8. https://onlinelibrary.wiley.com/doi/10.1002/ 9781118766804.wbiect220.

Borgman, Albert (2003). *Holding onto Reality: The Nature of Information at the Beginning of the 21st Century.* Chicago, IL: University of Chicago Press.

Borgmann, Albert (2003). *Power Failure: Christianity in the Culture of Technology.* Grand Rapids, MI: Baker Books.

Bostron, Nick (2003). The Transhumanist FAQ. https://nickbostrom.com/ views/transhumanist.pdf.

Bostrom, Nick (2014). *Superintelligence: Paths, Dangers, Strategies.* Oxford University Press. www.google.de/books/edition/Superintelligence/ 7_H8AwAAQBAJ?hl=en&gbpv=1&dq=Nick+Bostrom&printsec=frontcover.

Boynton, Andrew, & Milazzo, G. Tom (1996). Post-Fordist debate: A theoretical perspective to information technology and the firm. *Accounting, Management and Information Technologies, 6*(3), 157–173.

Bruce, Robert (1973). *Alexander Graham Bell and the Conquest of Solitude.* Ithaca: Cornell University Press.

Bunt, Gary R. (2009). *iMuslims: Rewiring the House of Islam.* New York City: The Other Press.

Campbell, Heidi (2009). Posthumanism. In Heidi Campbell & Heather Looy, eds., *The Science and Religion Primer,* Grand Rapids, MI: Baker Academic Books, 177–179.

Campbell, Heidi & LaPastina, Antonio (2010). How the iPhone became divine: Blogging, religion and intertextuality. *New Media and Society, 12*(7), 1191–1207. https://doi.org/10.1177/1461444810362204.

Campbell, Heidi A. (2006). Postcyborg ethics: A new way to speak of technology. *Explorations in Media Ecology, 5*(4), 279–296. https://doi.org/ 10.1386/eme.5.4.279_1.

Campbell, Heidi (2010). *When Religion Meets New Media.* New York: Routledge.

Campbell, Heidi (2013). The rise of the study of digital religion. In Campbell, H. ed., *Digital Religion. Understanding Religious Practice in New Media Worlds,* London: Routledge, 1–22.

Campbell, Heidi (2016). Problematizing the human-technology relationship through techno-spiritual myths presented in The Machine, Transcendence and Her. *Journal of Religion & Film, 20*(1). https://digitalcommons.uno maha.edu/jrf/vol20/iss1/21.

Campbell, Heidi (2016b). Framing the human-technology relationship: How Religious Digital Creatives engage posthuman narratives. *Social Compass, 63*(3), 302–318.

Campbell, Heidi (2021). How church online during the COVID-19 pandemic created space for a posthuman worldview. *Concilium, 3*, 43–54.

Campbell, Heidi, & Jones, Grace (2022). When the church embraced a posthuman future: How pastoral negotiations with technology during the Covid-19 pandemic resulted in an implicit acceptance of posthumanism. In *Postdigital Theologies: Technology, Belief, and Practice*, Cham: Springer.

Campbell, Heidi, & Tsuria, Ruth (2021). *Digital Religion, Understanding Religious Practice in Digital Media*. London: Routledge.

Cardwell, Mike (1996). *Dictionary of Psychology*. Chicago: Fitzroy Dearborn.

Carlson, Matt (2016). *Automated journalism: A posthuman future for digital news?* The Routledge companion to digital journalism studies, Routledge.

Carter, Allison (2023). "AI is your partner, not your secret": Making use of your "digital doppelganger," *PR Daily*. www.prdaily.com/ai-is-your-partner-not-your-secret-making-use-of-your-digital-doppelganger/.

Cassidy, Lance (2023). *How Generative AI Puts the Magic Back in Hardware Design*. EDN Network. www.edn.com/how-generative-ai-puts-the-magic-back-in-hardware-design/.

Castells, Manuel (1997). An introduction to the information age. *City, 2*(7), 6–16. https://doi.org/10.1080/13604819708900050.

Chen, Carolyn (2022). *Work Pray Code: When Work Becomes Religion in Silicon Valley*. New Jersey: Princeton University Press.

Coeckelbergh, Mark (2017.) *New Romantic Cyborgs: Romanticism, Information, Technology, and the End of the Machine*. Boston: MIT Press.

Cohen, Margaret (1989). Walter Benjamin's Phantasmagoria, *New German Critique, 48*, 87–107. https://doi.org/10.2307/488234.

Cole-Turner, Ron (2022). Posthumanism and transhumanism, In William Schweiker, ed., *Encyclopedia of Religious Ethics*, Hoboken, NJ: John Wiley & Sons, 1098–1105.

Hadden, Jeffery K., & Cowan, Douglas. E. (Eds.). (2000). *Religion on the Internet: Research prospects and promises*. New York: JAI. Sociology of Religion, 63, https://dio.org/10.2307/3712307.

Davis, Erik (1998). *Techgnosis*. New York: Harmony Books.

Dawkins, Richard (1976). *The Selfish Gene*. England: Oxford University Press.

Dembski, William A. (2002). *Intelligent Design: The Bridge Between Science Theology.* Lisle, IL: InterVarsity Press.

De Vreese, Claus. H. (2005). News framing: Theory and typology. *Information Design Journal+ Document Design, 13*(1), 51–62. https://doi.org/10.1075/idjdd.13.1.06vre.

DiTommaso, Lorenzo (2011). Apocalyptic eschatology and the transcendence of death in William Gibson's neuromancer. *The Journal of the Faculty of Religious Studies*, 37–54.

Eisenstein, Elizabeth (1980).*The Printing Press as an Agent of Change.* Cambridge, UK: Cambridge University Press, www.google.de/search?hl=de&tbo=p&tbm=bks&q=inauthor:%22Elizabeth+L.+Eisenstein%22.

Ellul, Jacques (1964). *The Technological Society.* New York: Alfred A. Knopf.

Esposito, John. L. (2018). *Islam: The Straight Path* (5th ed.). Oxford, UK: Oxford University Press.

Farisco, Michele (2013). Posthuman condition. In John Esposito, ed., *Encyclopedia of Sciences and Religions*, Dordrecht: Springer. https://doi.org/10.1007/978-1-4020-8265-8_1702.

Ferrando, Francesca (2013). Posthumanism, transhumanism, antihumanism, metahumanism, and new materialisms: Differences and relations. *Existenz, 8*(2), 26–32.

Ferrando, Francesca (2019). The posthuman divine: When robots can be enlightened. *SOPHIA, 58*, 645–651. https://doi.org/10.1007/s11841-019-00753-9.

Flood, Gavin (1996). *An introduction to Hinduism.* Cambridge University Press.

Flood, Gavin, & Martin, Charles (translators) (2013). *The Bhagavad Gita: A New Translation.* New York City: Penguin Classics.

Fox, Nick, & Alldred, Pam (2020). Re-assembling climate change policy: Materialism, posthumanism, and the policy assemblage. *The British Journal of Sociology, 71*(2), 268–283. https://doi.org/10.1111/1468-4446.12734.

Genovese, Andrea & Pansera, Mario (2019). *The Circular Economy at a Crossroad: Technocratic Eco-Modernism or Convivial Technology for Social Revolution?* https://ssrn.com/abstract=3459180 or http://dx.doi.org/10.2139/ssrn.3459180.

George, Susan (2006). *Religion and Technology in the 21st Century: Faith in the E-World.* Hershey, PA: Information Science.

Gibson, William (1984). *Neuromancer.* New York City: Ace Books.

Giddens, Anthony (1991). *Modernity and Self-Identity: Self and Society in the Late Modern Age.* Cambridge, UK: Polity.

Graham, Elaine (2002). *Representations of the Post/Human: Monsters, Aliens and Others in Popular Culture*. Manchester, UK: Manchester University Press.

Graham, Elaine (2015). The final frontier? Religion and posthumanism in film and television. In *The Palgrave Handbook of Posthumanism in Film and Television*, London, UK: Palgrave Macmillan, 361–370.

Greil, Arthur L. (1993). Exploration along the sacred frontier: Notes on para-religions, quasi-religions, and other boundary phenomena. In Hadden, Jeffrey. K. & Cowan, Douglas. E. eds., *The Handbook on Cults and Sects in America*, Leeds, UK: Emerald Group Publishing Limited, 305–323.

Grieve, Greg P., & Veidlinger, Daniel. (eds.). (2014). *Buddhism, the Internet, and Digital Media: The Pixel in the Lotus*. New York City: Routledge.

Grusin, Richard (eds.,) (2015). *The Nonhuman Turn*. Minneapolis, MN: University of Minnesota Press.

Hales, Kathryn (1999). *How We Became Posthuman: Virtual Bodies in Cybernetics, Literature, and Informatics*. Chicago, IL: Chicago University Press.

Hall, David (1997). *Lived Religion In America: Toward A History Of Practice*. Princeton, NJ: Princeton University Press.

Han, Sam (2016). *Technologies of Religion: Spheres of the Sacred in a Post-secular Modernity*. London: Routledge.

Haraway, Donna (1991). *Simians, Cyborgs, and Women: The Reinvention of Nature*. New York: Routledge.

Harvey, Peter (2013). *An Introduction to Buddhism: Teachings, History, and Practices* (2nd ed.). Cambridge, UK: Cambridge University Press.

Hauskeller, Michael, Philbeck, Thomas & Carbonell, Curtis (2015). *Posthumanism in Film and Television*. London, UK: Palgrave Macmillan UK.

Heidegger, Martin (1958). *The Question of Being*. Landham, MD: Rowman & Littlefield.

Heidegger, Martin (1977). *The Question Concerning Technology and Other Essays*, Lovitt W., trans., New York: Harper Torchbooks.

Illich, Ivan (1973/2021). *Tools of Conviviality.* London, UK: Marion Boyars.

Jaeger, Werner (1944). *Paideia: The Ideals of Greek Culture* (Vol. 1). Oxford, UK: Oxford University Press.

Jantzen, Grace (1995). *God's World, God's Body*. Louisville, KY: Westminster John Knox Press.

Kelly, Kevin (2010). *What Technology Wants*. New York: Penguin Books.

Kennedy, Eithne (2023). *Letter: Humanity Surpasses AI in Creativity and Spirituality*, Financial Times Opinion. www.ft.com/content/6028acf5-772d-4853-97a5-3459acbbd5bb.

Kingwell, Mark (2022). *Singular Creatures: Robots, Rights, and the Politics of Posthumanism*. Montreal, QC: McGill Queen's University Press.

Kingwell, Mark (2023). *Why are we so afraid of being displaced by machines? It's only human nature*, Toronto Globe and Mail online. www.theglobeand mail.com/opinion/article-why-are-we-so-afraid-of-being-displaced-by-machines-its-only-human/.

Kline, Ronald (2003). Resisting consumer technology in rural America: The telephone and electrification. *Technology and Culture, 44*(4), 759–790. https://doi.org/10.1353/tech.2003.0202.

Koetsier, John (2023). *Ray Kurzweil On AI Pause: No*, Forbes.com. www .forbes.com/sites/johnkoetsier/2023/05/08/ray-kurzweil-on-ai-pause-no/ amp/.

Kurzweil, Ray (1999). *The Age of Spiritual Machines: When Computers Exceed Human Intelligence*. London: Penguin Books.

Lee, Brant T. (2007). The devil in the details: An essay on the blind watchmaker, the invisible hand, and the theology of whiteness. *Quinnipiac Law Review, 26*, 7–6.

Levenson, John. D. (2006). *The love of God: Divine gift, human gratitude, and mutual faithfulness in Judaism*. Princeton, NJ: Princeton University Press.

Lim, Alvin (2018). *Digital Spirits in Religion and Media: Possession and Performance*. London: Routledge. www.routledge.com/Digital-Spirits-in-Religion-and-Media-Possession-and-Performance/Lim/p/book/ 9780815393320.

Lövheim, Mia (2013). Young people, religious identity, and the internet. In Morten Hojsgaard & Margit Warburg, eds., *Religion Online*. London, UK: Routledge, 59–74.

Luckmann, Thomas (1967). *The Invisible Religion: The Problem of Religion in Modern Society*. New York City: New York University.

MacKenzie, Donald (1984). Marx and the machine. *Technology and culture, 25* (3), 473–502.

Martin, Joel (2017). *Edison vs. Tesla: The Battle over Their Last Invention*. New York City: Simon and Schuster.

Marx, Karl (1867). *Machinery and Large-Scale Industry: Volume 1*. Moscow: Progress Publishers. www.marxists.org/archive/marx/works/download/pdf/ Capital-Volume-I.pdf.

Marx, Karl (1975). *Collected Works* (Vol. I). New York: International.

McArthur, Neil (2023). *Gods in the machine? The rise of artificial intelligence may result in new religions*, The Conversation. https://theconversation.com/ gods-in-the-machine-the-rise-of-artificial-intelligence-may-result-in-new-religions-201068.

McCutcheon, Russell (2018). *Studying Religion: An Introduction*. London: Routledge.

McGrath, Alister (2011). *Christian Theology: An Introduction* (5th ed.). Hoboken, NJ: Wiley-Blackwell.

McLeod, Saul (2015). Stereotypes. www.simplypsychology.org/katz-braly.html

McOmber, James B. (1999). Technological autonomy and three definitions of technology. *Journal of Communication*, *49*(3), 137–153.

Mitcham, Carl (1986). Computers: From ethos and ethics to mythos and religion. *Technology in Society*, 8(3), 171–201.

Mitcham, Carl (1994). Thinking through technology. In *The Path Between Engineering and Philosophy*. Epilogue, Chicago, IL: University of Chicago Press. www.compilerpress.ca/Competitiveness/Anno/Anno%20Mitcham%20TTT%202%20Epil.htm.

Mitcham, Carl (2022). Technology as a Theological Problem in the Christian Tradition. In Carl Mitchum, James Grote, & Levi Checketts, eds., *Theology and Technology, Volume 1: Essays in Christian Analysis, 1*. London, UK: Perlego, 1–17.

Mitcham, Carl, Grote, Jim, & Checketts, Levi (2022). *Theology and Technology, Volume 1* [Edition unavailable]. Wipf and Stock Publishers. https://www.perlego.com/book/3570594/theology-and-technology-volume-1-essays-in-christian-analysis-pdf.

Mitcham, Carl & Mackey, Robert (1971). Jacques Ellul and the technological society. *Philosophy Today*, *15*(2), 102.

Murray, Lisa (2023). PODCAST: *The race to God-like AI and what it means for humanity*, Financial Review. www.afr.com/technology/the-race-to-god-like-ai-and-what-it-means-for-humanity-20230614-p5dgji.

NA (2012). Atelier: Demonic Technologies: Walter Benjamin and the Return of Religion in the Study of Technology [workshop], Intempestif Walter Benjamin Blog. https://intempestifbenjamin.wordpress.com/2012/04/24/atelier-demonic-technologies-walter-benjamin-and-the-return-of-religion-in-the-study-of-technology-harvard-27-avril-2012/.

Noble, David (1999). *The Religion of Technology: The Divinity of Man and the Spirit of Invention*. New York: Penguin.

Oldenburg, Ray (1997). Our vanishing third places. *Planning Commissioners Journal*, 25(4), 6–10.

Ong, Walter (2012). *Rhetoric, Romance, and Technology: Studies in the Interaction of Expression and Culture*. New York: Cornell University Press.

Padgett, Alan (2005). God versus technology? Science, secularity, and the theology of technology. *Zygon*, 40(3), 577–584. https://doi.org/10.1111/j.1467-9744.2005.00689.x.

Pepperell, Robert (1995). *The Posthuman Condition*. Exeter: Intellect Books.

Pepperell, Robert (2005). *The Posthuman Manifesto*. www.intertheory.org/pep perell.htm.

Peters, John D. (1999). *Speaking into the Air: A History of the Idea of Communication*. Chicago, IL: Chicago University Press.

Pivetti, Massimo (2015). Marx and the development of critical political economy. *Review of Political Economy*, *27*(2), 134–153.

Plato (1997). *The Republic*. (G. M. A. Grube, Trans.). Hackett.

Principe, Walter (1983). Toward defining spirituality. *Studies in Religion/ Sciences Religieuses*, *12*(2), 127–141.

Robinson, Richard (1969). *Plato's Earlier Dialectic*. Oxford University Press.

Robinson, Brett. T. (2013). *Appletopia: Media Technology and the Religious Imagination of Steve Jobs*. Waco, TX: Baylor University.

Roden, David (2015). *Posthuman Life: Philosophy on the Edge of the Human*. London: Routledge.

Roobeek, Annemieke J. M. (1987). The crisis in Fordism and the rise of a new technological paradigm. *Futures*, 19(2), 129–154.

Rose, Steve (July 6, 2023). *Five Ways AI Could Improve the World: "We Can Cure All Diseases, Stabilise Our Climate, Halt Poverty,"* The Guardian. www.theguardian.com/technology/2023/jul/06/ai-artificial-intelligence-world-diseases-climate-scenarios-experts.

Salomon, Jean-Jacques (1984). What is technology? The Issue of its origins and definitions. *History and Technology, an International Journal*, *1*(2), 113–156.

Samuel, Sigal (September 7, 2023). Silicon Valley's vision for AI? It's religion, repackaged. *Vox online*. www.vox.com/the-highlight/23779413/silicon val leys-ai-religion-transhumanism-longtermism-ea.

Schatzberg, Eric (2006). Technik comes to America: Changing meanings of technology before 1930. *Technology and Culture*, *47*(3), 486–512. https://doi.org/10.1353/tech.2006.0132.

Shelley, Mary (2018). *Frankenstein: The 1818 Text*. New York City: Penguin.

Singler, Beth (2020). "Blessed by the algorithm"; Theistic conceptions of artificial intelligence in online discourse. *AI & Society*, 35, 945–955.

Sorgner, Stefan Lorenz. (2010). Beyond humanism: Reflections on trans-and posthumanism. *Journal of Evolution and Technology*, *21*(2), 1–19.

St. Lawrence, Emma (2023). *TikTok, Technomancy & the Rise of Algorithmic Divination*. Conference Presentation at the International Society of Media, Religion & Culture: Bochum, Germany.

Stahl, William (1999). *God and the Chip: Religion and the Culture of Technology*. Waterloo, ON: Wilfred Laurier University Press.

Standage, Thomas (2014). *The Victorian Internet: The Remarkable Story of the Telegraph and the Nineteenth Century's On-Line Pioneers*. London: Bloomsbury.

Taylor, Josh & Hern, Alex (May 2, 2023). *"Godfather of AI" Geoffrey Hinton Quits Google and Warns Over Dangers of Misinformation*. The Guardian Online. https://amp.theguardian.com/technology/2023/may/02/geoffrey-hinton-godfather-of-ai-quits-google-warns-dangers-of-machine-learning.

Veblen, Thorstein (1921). *The Engineers and the Price System*. New York: B. W. Huebsch.

Wanjiru, Roseline (2015). Fordist Production. In Frederick F. Wherry & Juliet B. Schor, eds., *The SAGE Encyclopedia of Economics and Society, Vol. 1*, Thousand Oaks, CA: SAGE Publications, 708–709.

Warwick, Kevin (2002). *I, Cyborg*. Ottawa, ON: Century Press.

Weaver, David A., Lively, Erica, & Bimber, Bruce (2009). Searching for a frame: News media tell the story of technological progress, risk, and regulation. *Science Communication*, 31(2), 139–166.

Whitman, James Q. (2004). The two western cultures of privacy: Dignity versus liberty, Faculty Scholarship Series, 113, 1151–221, Paper 649, http://digitalcommons.law.yale.edu/fss_papers/649.

Wilkinson, John (1964). Translator's introduction. In Ellul, Jacques, ed., *The Technological Society*, New York: Alfred A. Knopf, Inc., ix–xx.

Zeiler, Xenia. (ed.). (2019). *Digital Hinduism*. New York: Routledge.

Cambridge Elements ≡

The Problems of God

Series Editor
Michael L. Peterson
Asbury Theological Seminary

Michael L. Peterson is Professor of Philosophy at Asbury Theological Seminary. He is the author of *God and Evil* (Routledge); *Monotheism, Suffering, and Evil* (Cambridge University Press); *With All Your Mind* (University of Notre Dame Press); *C. S. Lewis and the Christian Worldview* (Oxford University Press); *Evil and the Christian God* (Baker Book House); and *Philosophy of Education: Issues and Options* (Intervarsity Press). He is co-author of *Reason and Religious Belief* (Oxford University Press); *Science, Evolution, and Religion: A Debate about Atheism and Theism* (Oxford University Press); and *Biology, Religion, and Philosophy* (Cambridge University Press). He is editor of *The Problem of Evil: Selected Readings* (University of Notre Dame Press). He is co-editor of *Philosophy of Religion: Selected Readings* (Oxford University Press) and *Contemporary Debates in Philosophy of Religion* (Wiley-Blackwell). He served as General Editor of the Blackwell monograph series Exploring Philosophy of Religion and is founding Managing Editor of the journal *Faith and Philosophy*.

About the Series

This series explores problems related to God, such as the human quest for God or gods, contemplation of God, and critique and rejection of God. Concise, authoritative volumes in this series will reflect the methods of a variety of disciplines, including philosophy of religion, theology, religious studies, and sociology.

For EU product safety concerns, contact us at Calle de José Abascal, 56–1°,
28003 Madrid, Spain or eugpsr@cambridge.org.